SOCIAL MARKETING SUCCESS

Seb Brantigan
The Britpreneur

Copyright © 2020 Seb Brantigan

All rights reserved.

ISBN:

DEDICATION

First, I wish to mention a few great people that have helped me to grow my business and taught me some important lessons about being an entrepreneur. Not only that, but they have saved me from making some costly and probably very embarrassing mistakes early on. They have contributed to the lessons and strategies that led to this book being written, hence it's only fair to give them a mention.

James Nicholson

For showing me the ropes when it comes to building a digital business online. I have learnt more in a matter of months working with him, than I did previously spending years trying to do everything on my own. I made so many mistakes going solo that I know wouldn't have happened if I had been working with James sooner. He has also kept me accountable and not let me make excuses to avoid improving my business. James, you have certainly helped me to fast track my results with Internet Marketing and I am forever grateful.

Darren Little

His talents when it comes to understanding people and empowering them to get results are second to none. I've also never seen someone so dedicated to getting people to their personal and business breakthroughs. I remember flying all the way out to Nashville, Tennessee just to meet you at an event! It was well worth the trip and I got more value from having one lunch with you than I did across the whole event.

When it comes to social media, he certainly knows his stuff and has shared some great knowledge with me on how to grow your business using it. Thank you, Darren, for your commitment and time mentoring me on all areas of business and leadership marketing.

Sam Druce

For endlessly 'talking shop' with me, sending some fantastic opportunities in my direction and also a great mentor in a lot of ways. There have been a number of times I've been stuck with something marketing related that I haven't come across before, and he has been there to point me in the right direction every time. A very reliable guy in business and as a friend. Thank you for being you Sam.

Mike Dillard

When I started to market online and was getting completely lost, Mike helped me with the power of Attraction Marketing from the lessons in his book 'Magnetic Sponsoring'. This is the art of getting people to chase you down, instead of you chasing others. I faced a lot of rejection until he taught me how Attraction Marketing works and it's something that has stuck with me ever since. Mike taught me the power of removing neediness and giving value, which has helped my business grow so much quicker. I can't thank you enough for these crucial lessons.

CONTENTS

DEDICATION 3

BONUS 1:
5 DAY SOCIAL MARKETING SUCCESS CHALLENGE 9

CHAPTER 1.
INTRODUCTION TO SOCIAL
MARKETING SUCCESS 11

   YOU DON'T NEED TO BE A TECHNICAL WIZARD
   WHY DID I WRITE THIS BOOK?
   THE POWER OF SOCIAL MEDIA

CHAPTER 2.
WHY SOCIAL MEDIA AND WHY NOW? 18

   SOCIAL MEDIA VS TRADITIONAL MEDIA
   PITFALLS AND RISKS OF SOCIAL MEDIA
   STRENGTHS OF SOCIAL MEDIA

CHAPTER 3.
WHO I AM AND WHAT YOU
CAN LEARN FROM ME? 26

   SEB, THE BRITPRENEUR
   GOING FULLTIME WITH SOCIAL AND DIGITAL MARKETING
   ME, AT THIS MOMENT IN TIME

CHAPTER 4.
WHAT CAN SOCIAL MARKETING
SUCCESS DO FOR YOU?

   GETTING STARTED
   VALUE OF SOCIAL MEDIA IN BUSINESS
   WHAT YOU WILL LEARN?

CHAPTER 5.
THE OLD AND THE NEW   41

MAKE SOCIAL MEDIA WORK FOR YOU: GAIN CLIENTS & LEADS
AUDIENCE AND DIGITAL ASSET GROWTH
THE VALUE OF A SOCIAL MEDIA AUDIENCE

CHAPTER 6.
WHAT YOU SHOULD BE POSTING   45

DON'T OVER COMPLICATE
CONTENT: GAIN MAXIMUM EXPOSURE FOR YOUR BUSINESS
FACEBOOK BUSINESS PAGES AND GROUPS

CHAPTER 7.
AN INTRODUCTION TO THE FOUR STEP FORMULA   61

INTRODUCTION TO THE FORMULA

CHAPTER 8.
PLATFORM (THE EASY AUDIENCE FINDER PLAN)   65

RECOMMENDED PLATFORMS
PLATFORM OVERVIEW
WHICH IS BEST FOR YOU?

CHAPTER 9.
IDENTIFY (THE PERFECT CLIENT SOLUTION)   68

DEFINE YOUR CUSTOMER
MAP OUT YOUR AVATAR

CHAPTER 10.
MESSAGE – (THE MAGNETIC CONTENT FORMULA)   72

CONTENT: GET CREATIVE
ENGAGE, DON'T HARD SELL

CHAPTER 11.
PROMOTION (THE RAPID EXPOSURE SYSTEM) 75

    POST OR NOT TO POST: CONSISTENCY IS THE KEY
    MARKETING V PRODUCT QUALITY
    DIRECT MESSAGING TIPS AND PITFALLS

CHAPTER 12.
WHAT TO AVOID   **81**

    CONTENT CATASTROPHES!
    AVOIDING TROLLS
    KEEP IT AUTHENTIC

CHAPTER 13.
WHAT IT TAKES TO GO VIRAL   **89**

    CREATIVE CONTENT FOR VIRAL CLICKS!

CHAPTER 14.
HOW TO SCALE YOUR BUSINESS UP   **93**

    GROWTH AND ENGAGEMENT TIPS
    LOOKING TO THE FUTURE
    PATIENCE = RESULTS, REWARDS

CHAPTER 15.   **YOUR NEXT STEPS**   **107**

    SQUASH YOUR FEARS
    LASER-FOCUSED
    PRODUCTIVITY TIPS

BONUS SECTION
COMPLIMENTARY SAMPLE COACHING BY THE BRITPRENEUR 113

RESOURCES   **115**

BONUS 1:
5 DAY SOCIAL MARKETING SUCCESS CHALLENGE

Before we go any further, if you bought this book directly from Amazon rather than my website, you may not know about this bonus I created for you as a valued Social Marketing Success book customer. To say thank you for buying the book, you can gain access to my 5 Day Social Marketing Success Challenge for free. It's designed to show you how to get more leads and sales using social media, and in each of the 5 days I'll walk you through one simple strategy to improve the results of your social media efforts. Plus, it's a perfect companion for the book that helps you to apply what you're learning.

If you haven't yet joined the Challenge, register below and I'll send you all the details right away:

https://sebbrantigan.net/smchallenge

Some feedback from previous training sessions:

"Seb's presentation was very worthwhile. Broken down into logical sections with practical advice throughout. The pace was spot on for the audience and actionable steps were offered to enable every participant to go away with an achievable plan of action." -Rachel Turner, EFT MRA / TFT Practitioner

"So excited because I love challenges, and this is definitely kicking it for me. I can't wait. I am proud of you. You're the youngest marketer on my FB and one of the highest potentials I've seen on here." Kristine Wiegand, Health Consultant

CHAPTER 1.

INTRODUCTION TO SOCIAL MARKETING SUCCESS

"What if..."

I wondered to myself.

What if there was a social media book that could take someone who is brand new to social media and quickly get them exposure to their business or brand?

What if you didn't need to be a technical wizard or have lots of business experience to still use social media to get more leads, sales, and clients?

To date, I haven't read very many thorough social media books that achieved these steps, so I decided to write the book 'Social Marketing Success'. Your support in buying this book is truly appreciated. Without it, my message would not impact anyone, so by investing in this book you really are making my visions and goals a reality. Also, if you bought a book for someone else, you are impacting them too, so I'm very grateful if you also told a friend, family member or colleague about the book.

Before I get into the chapters of the book, I wanted to say a massive thank you. Not just for grabbing a copy but also for actually reading it. The last thing I want is to contribute to a 'shelf help' society that buys books they don't read.

It's the same with digital products and eBooks too. While this book might double up as a drinks mat, it certainly won't do your business or brand any favours if you don't implement what's being taught. I'm not in the business of being dishonest so I'll admit that I still do this from time to time! We are all human... However, you will definitely get out what you put in with this book.

Thanks again for getting stuck in and making a start, even if you're a slow reader like me. I've put in my absolute best effort to make it worth your time and only included information that I feel is going to get you results.

I've gone through this book rigorously to make sure anything that doesn't meet that criteria hasn't made it to the finished result. Many late nights went into making this the best possible book for someone who is either new to using social media for business or has struggled to get any results.

Now, you might be wondering why did I write this book in the first place?

There are several good reasons for this...

Firstly, I have had the idea for Social Marketing Success in my head for a long time, and it feels good to finally share it with the world. Especially when you have a lot of people asking you for social media advice - you may have even contributed to this book without knowing it!

Secondly, a smaller factor but still something worth mentioning, is at the time of writing this book the world is recovering from a pandemic and the effect it created will be remembered for generations. Experts say that just the economic impact alone will likely take over a decade to return to how things were before the outbreak.

Before you start to wonder if you are still actually reading a book on social media, you'll hear me explain why this is relevant to social media shortly. There is a connection between this and the power of social media which I feel is important to mention.

The pandemic I'm referring to is called the COVID-19 (Coronavirus), which by now you and virtually every human on Earth has heard of. I won't waste time explaining it as you can Google if you want to learn the specifics (even though you aren't short to find information about it in the Press), but the disease led to governments around the world, including ours in the UK, enforcing a lockdown preventing anyone from leaving the house unless essential.

It's created a new way of living for all of us, with many businesses that went back to work not returning to an office, but instead hiring hotel rooms for their meetings. Others, that faced closing their doors, have adapted their businesses so that everything can be done online.

Most importantly, it's a great example of why you should be looking to take your business and make it run entirely online wherever possible. Even traditional businesses need to look at new ways to innovate their enterprise or they will simply be left behind.

Thanks to the power of technology, I'm able to run my business without any serious interruptions. This is because everything I do is online or over the phone; face to face is useful for certain projects but not essential.

Like many business owners, my 'corner of the bedroom' home office is where it all started. In fact, some of the most successful online marketers I know still work from home, instead of from an oversized corporate office.

However, many businesses struggled during the lockdown, as they were not allowed to physically hold business meetings, even one-to-one potential client meetings due to government advice.

That said, some businesses were smart and adapted quickly, such as networking and growing their business online. For example, I currently work with events-based businesses that only run online events, and no longer want to return to in-person events (except for 1 to 1 clients or small groups). In a way this actually has increased their value, as you don't get to work closely with the team unless you pay for the opportunity.

Things are getting back to normal somewhat but the situation has poked a huge hole in many business models that probably needed to change at some point anyway.

Moving on, what kind of influence has that had on this book?

It goes without saying that the outbreak gave me more time to write this book! Whilst this has not been a positive experience for anyone, I'm willing to bet it has taught us some lessons and changed our outlook on certain things. Sometimes it takes something drastic to bring us to our senses. An interesting observation is that people have mainly stayed in touch by using mediums such as social media. So, if this is where the majority of peoples' attention is, your business should also feature there too.

Yes, I realise that not every business can run their entire operation online, however in the digital marketing world doing everything online is the norm. Even if you had a shop in a specific location you could advertise to people online about it. For these types of business models, they were virtually unaffected by the crisis and some actually did better as a result of it. Some businesses were thriving to the point that they refused millions of pounds in entitled government aid for furloughed employees.

Unfortunately, not all companies were quite so lucky as most either had to make lots of staff redundant or close up shop completely. Some business models are more adaptable than others, however virtually all businesses could do something to adapt. For example, I've seen nightclubs change their layouts and open as bars instead to abide by government regulations. Many companies that were only operating offline have moved entirely online and closed their shops. It's where the majority of your customers are anyway.

What this shows is that even during one of the deepest recessions the Internet still thrives - the only exception I can think of is the Dot-com Bubble. At a time when people are said to 'have no money' and there are millions of job losses, there are others in the marketplace outdoing themselves. For example, where some businesses are folding there are always investors looking to buy them out and take over.

Where does social media come into this?

A relevant example of this is an entrepreneur called Tai Lopez, who has relentlessly been posting on social media platforms like Snapchat and Instagram. He has millions of followers across all his social media channels and does cool things not many influencers do, like cash giveaways.

If you haven't heard of this guy, he does get a lot of criticism, however Tai and his business partner bought a few 'giants' that were about to go under such as 131-year old retail chain, Modell's Sporting Goods*. They even did a post dedicated to their haters, to let them know they aren't just posting on social media and are building real businesses. This is a great lesson that today's economy does not have to be YOUR personal economy.

Every person I know (including the 'boomer' generation) has access to social media, which has become the distribution centre for much of the information we see every day. Traditional newspapers have become a thing of the past now that we can pick and choose our news online.

Yes, there are still platforms such as blogs and news articles but mostly these end up being discussed on social media. Even emails - which aren't as easy to share on social media - become shared by others if they are interesting enough or forwarded privately via platforms such as Messenger or WhatsApp.

*Source - Forbes:

https://www.forbes.com/sites/joanverdon/2020/08/23/the-name-game-why-tai-lopez-and-alex-mehr-bought-modells-and-other-retail-brands/#461499b32199

How should you use this book?

I only have two suggestions here; read the chapters in order and read them with an open mind. Some of the information and strategies in this book might contradict what you're currently doing or have learnt before. These are of course strategies that have worked for me, but make sure to follow them whilst adding your own 'personal flair' for the best results.

What you want to avoid is copying mine or anyone's personality. Doing so will eventually get you in trouble. As we are each unique and people are clever and will spot if you're being authentic or not! Take your 'personal flair' and learn how to broadcast this on social media. We'll cover how you can do this in Social Marketing Success, but let me ask a huge question that often gets asked.

CHAPTER 2.

WHY SOCIAL MEDIA AND WHY NOW?

It doesn't matter what type of business you have, almost every business will benefit quickly from using social media. Traditional businesses that don't process any online orders can drive potential customers to place an order. Local businesses can also benefit, no longer relying on footfall or referrals alone.

If you're neither and are a charity, nonprofit or social enterprise, then guess what? Social Media can work for these kinds of organisations too. Of course, the objective will be different if you are a charity, for example, but that doesn't mean you must miss out on the action. You might have a different message or offer to share, but the principles remain the same.

If we compare social media to other advertising platforms such as TV, radio, and magazine advertising, it is much easier and more cost effective to set up. Advertising on social media is much more targeted and brings traffic to your website faster. You don't have to hire expensive copywriters, graphics designers, project managers and who knows what else, to get the job done. No more waiting for weeks to get an advert approved and running by a publisher or a media buyer, take back control and do it yourself... starting today!

The best way I can describe using social media for business, is that it's similar to a giant meetup group. If you're there for business you are probably going to want to network, however there's an important fact to remember.

People are not on social media to make a purchase, so they won't like being sold to! Doing so would be like proposing on the first date. People are predominantly on social media for entertainment. Someone who wants to catch up with friends or family, play FarmVille or 'poke' someone they shamelessly fancy (yes, Facebook still has a 'poke' feature)! People aren't sitting in front of their computers or smartphones with their credit card in hand ready to buy.

That said, people DO like to buy but they don't like to be sold to via social media. Treating it like a noticeboard will not help your business because the success of your content relies on engagement. No engagement (new likes and comments, etc) will leave your social media accounts looking unloved which does not give a great first impression. Plus, the longer your content goes without engagement, the harder it is to rebuild it. Similar to exercise, if you engage with your customers every day or close to daily, it doesn't seem like hard work but becomes part of your daily routine.

The art of getting people to buy who don't like being sold to, is to create enticing and useful content to attract their attention. Don't worry if this seems like an overwhelming task, we're going to break it down together in this book in a step by step process. In fact, it's a lot easier than trying to sell by convincing someone, as you're going to learn the art of selling without being pushy. It is selling without traditional sales techniques, as these usually face a lot of resistance and rejection. Importantly, you're also going to learn how to get your message in front of the right people. I have created a four-step process on exactly how this works, which will be explained within this book.

I'm not for a moment suggesting that social media is the only marketing strategy that gets results, traditional media can still work really well for certain types of businesses. In most cases, as mentioned at the start of the book, it is not very accessible for startups. It requires more regulations to follow so using it to create a marketing campaign could be time intensive.

One exception, of which I'm a customer of, is a print newsletter which due to the audience it's aimed at is deliberately in print rather than digital. It's fun to receive things in the post because it is so rare nowadays. I'm quite sure we don't get as excited at seeing an email or a Facebook status! Simply because there are pages and pages of it, you could spend a whole day looking at content on social media and never get through half of it.

Mediums such as print advertising can still be effective, and they have worked for a very long time. That said, these traditional advertising methods are on the decline due to the vast amount of online marketing strategies available for business owners to use.

Many of these newer strategies are low (or even zero) cost to get started with, which pushes more 'archaic' methods like print or even phone calls to the back of the pile. Platforms that now offer advertising to over a billion people were once called a 'fad' and criticized by many. It's fair to say that they are no longer a fad and are here to stay.

The use of social media has been instrumental for newer businesses, however it does not come without its drawbacks. As great as social media is, I want to be transparent with you from the start and let you know these exist.

Unfortunately, some businesses are just not using it correctly or even at all. Using it the wrong way or not at all can actually make your business look bad, even if you already have an existing social media presence. Having a social media account that you barely post on makes it look like you don't care about your audience or your business. It makes you appear like you have nothing interesting to say!

One example of this, referring back to the lockdown, was a pub I would frequent that offered takeaway beer and cider. The only issue is that I learnt about this by word of mouth, not by social media as their Facebook page hadn't been updated for years. This meant that I had to go and visit their noticeboard (during lockdown!) outside the pub to check availability. Hardly an ideal way to sell a product that literally sells itself!

It would be so easy for a pub to create content on how to make cider, for example. Or even talk about their favourite beer and why they like it so much. There are content creators on platforms like YouTube already doing this that have millions of followers. You won't make much money in the short term from this of course, but people will remember you. It's a ten-minute job maximum, and something you could document or video whilst doing your normal duties.

This is why many business owners with similar thinking fail; they aren't thinking long term and so they don't last long term, especially when things change. Also, they rest on their laurels and tend to get complacent just because they have an audience elsewhere. They think that they don't have to continually put in effort, which in the short term may be true. However, in the long term, it's the business owner that keeps showing up with consistent content that gets the most exposure (and thus the most customers).

One pub I saw really capitalising on this during lockdown continued their weekly pub quiz on Instagram. If my business was shut with no income coming in, and I had time on my hands, then I would be doing something like this just to keep busy!

If you're not sure what content is and this term is new to you, I'll be talking about content by sharing different types and examples of content you can use later in the book.

One other battle with social media is that illegitimate profiles and pages can also be set up - pretending to be other people or businesses - or to phish for people's information.

Unfortunately, scammers can create social media accounts without even needing to prove any formal identity. This also leaves you vulnerable to haters that may try to leave negative comments about your business.

Of course, this won't happen until you gain a lot of exposure on social media, so it's a good problem to have - at least your business is visible! In a lot of cases, there isn't much you can do here. Luckily, if you stay resilient these types of people will quickly go away and pick on someone less prepared. I'll touch on this in more detail later in the book.

Another potential issue to be aware of, is people may try to hack your account(s) and gain control of them. If they're successful and they manage to lock you out of your account, your business is at a huge disadvantage if you solely rely on social media.

I know people who have lost tens of thousands of friends or followers and have had to start over from scratch. I also know others who managed to regain access to their account, but it took them several weeks. Not everyone is that lucky, and if the rogue user starts posting on your account it might not be obvious to your customers that someone else is using your account. Even having a secure password is not full protection from hackers as these can still be hacked by someone determined enough to get into your account(s).

Platforms such as Facebook have also been open to information misuse as proven by the Cambridge Analytica fiasco in 2018. The personal data of up to 87 million Facebook users was acquired and shared without their consent or knowledge. Nope, I'm not trying to scare you away but by putting your information anywhere online this is a possibility down the line.

Later in this book I'll be sharing how to build audiences elsewhere, to make your business less vulnerable if something does happen on social media. While it is a great strategy, you should never put all your eggs in one basket in terms of where your leads or revenue comes from.

Using any social media platform does carry these risks, no matter how small, so it's important to be ever vigilant. While I don't want to put you off early on, I'm not in the business of giving false or unreal expectations so I'd rather you know now than be chasing your tail later. Just know that there is no platform completely immune to these problems and they can happen to anyone. The risks, however, I feel are quite insignificant compared to the pay off. My belief is that we already all have a lot less privacy than we think we have, but that's definitely a topic for another book!

With that said, I think that we can all agree technology has come a *very* long way. To the point that it's become part of our everyday lives, and we can't live without it very easily. For most of us, we definitely wouldn't be able to do our job without it.

Politicians have used Social Media to win elections. They may have even used it to find the love of their life or vice versa. If you're one of the ones that found out about Social Marketing Success on social media, then that's even bigger proof that it works. Best of all, you can be a part of it simply from the palm of your hand - using the power of your smartphone.

A lot of what you're reading is being written on my smartphone or tablet, rather than my laptop (most laptop keyboards I find difficult to use for extended periods of typing). Now you can even use a speak-to-text software to write an entire book.

I'm writing this on Google Docs which has this feature and many more useful built in. Even if you hated writing with a passion, you could speak content, articles, books, and other written information into existence - without actually writing a single word. This technology doesn't cost a penny to use so anybody can take advantage.

The flexibility of working in a way that suits you, gives you the upper hand to build a profitable business that hardly existed before the Internet. We are becoming a more mobile society with desktop PC users declining rapidly. You literally have an entire computer in your pocket or purse. Even if you're like me and prefer to work off a laptop, less and less people are using them to browse on social media.

It's no different with social media. We are very rarely more than two feet away from our phones and are always wanting to stay connected. It's just the way we live, so why not embrace it and capitalise on it. You and I both have the same opportunity to leverage this trend.

So before we get into how to really do that, how this book can benefit you, whatever stage you might be in your business or career…here's more about me in case you have no idea who I am.

CHAPTER 3.

WHO I AM AND WHAT YOU CAN LEARN FROM ME?

Now you might be wondering, well who actually am I and why should you listen to me over someone else with a similar message?

I'm known as The Britpreneur online because all the other cool names were taken! All jokes aside, I've been in the digital marketing world since 2010 so for a decade now. Yes, that is a genuine fact, as you can find content such as videos and articles dating back to 2010 if you look hard enough. Just Google my name and all the proof is there so browse away. I'm not making things up like a lot of gurus do and I'm a very open book. Anyway, how can you tell if I really know my stuff?

I've worked with TV celebrities, personal development authorities and supported seven-figure businesses from the ground up with their digital marketing. I know what it takes to go from zero to hero with social media and marketing your business online.

A huge part of my learning experience has been through doing trial and error. It's fair to say that I've tried almost everything there is to try when it comes to mastering social media.

While I don't have millions of followers on social media, it has generated for me more than enough long term clients and customers. It's allowed me to build a full-time income just from social media, so I feel very comfortable sharing how that works with you. It's all about quality not quantity. For example, I have worked with celebrities to help them to launch offers to their audiences (some with over 1 million followers), yet even with those numbers I have actually achieved more with smaller, more targeted audiences.

That said, I'm nobody special... there's nothing I'm doing here that you can't also do. There is however something special about the system I've created that you can replicate starting today. More importantly I'm still actively using what you're reading in this book; there's no outdated strategies here or anything taught I've not used myself. There are too many people sharing old information which is no longer effective and it's doing the digital marketing industry a lot of harm. Nope, you won't get anything of that sort from me. I also won't pretend to you that I know everything, but what I can share has already helped a lot of people.

In all honesty, how I got into online marketing is by pure chance, I didn't start with a lot of money or resources. This fell into my lap by accident while I was trying to figure out ways to make money online in my spare time.

The year was 2016 and I was working a nice steady government job, although on the side I was spending as much time as I could looking into a second stream of income. All I would see when I logged online is people making the magic amount of £10,000 per month on autopilot, whilst sitting on the beach sipping Sangrias and working 30 seconds a day. I've seen all the hype too many times now, but at the time I bought into anything that told me I could make lots of money.

Although making £10,000 per month wasn't my exact dream, the concept of making money in a more automated way gave me the 'Internet Marketing' bug. All I wanted to do was make enough money to cover my bills and go on holiday more than once a year. Yep I know, very unrealistic ambitions!

That said, the job I had was well paid for what I did, with plenty of holiday and sick pay. I also was working flexible hours, so it wasn't even a 9-to-5 most of the time, and the people I worked with were nice. Sometimes the hours were long, but all in all compared to other jobs you could say everything was going swimmingly.

Out of the blue our team was summoned to a meeting where we were informed about a restructure...jobs would be lost and some merged into others. Everyone had to reapply for their jobs which for me spelt the opportunity to move up and try for an Assistant Manager position...after all, I was a hard worker and surely my efforts would be realised. At last I could move up the corporate ladder!

So, I made my application and waited... a week passed.

At 9:07am, just as I sat down at my computer and the warm smell of cheap instant coffee hit me, an email went 'BING' in my inbox inviting me to a meeting at noon.

Heading to the 4th floor Executive-style glass meeting rooms, I had a feeling of confidence... like this was going to be 'my day'. I entered the meeting room and closed the heavy sliding door behind me. However, the atmosphere in the room was not so... inviting. In fact, you could sense something was up straight away. Ever heard the expression you can cut the atmosphere with a knife? It was all a bit awkward to say the least.

My Manager was there, along with her Manager, and the HR head of the restructure. Here's the first thing she said, with a worried look on her face:

"Seb, I'm sorry you were unsuccessful in your applications and we are going to have to start the redundancy process, meaning your position in the company will be terminated."

All of a sudden... I was being made redundant on the spot! Literally speechless, pretty much all I could think to shout was "What The F***"! ...but the only thing going through my head, was how was I going to pay my bills next month?

If you've ever had a moment where you're in literal shock and your heart sinks to your feet, that was me when I received this news. I hadn't been working there long enough to be given even a months' redundancy pay. What about savings to fall back on? Forget about it, I was already investing every last penny into online marketing.

Yep that's right, the most senior non-Manager in the team (who naively thought a promotion was coming his way) was slapped round the face and given 30 days' notice instead. Thanks for all your hard work, sorry you're not getting paid next month. Fun times!

Looking back, it was an unfair but humbling experience which taught me an invaluable business lesson. Never just rely on one source of income. And equally this also applies to not relying on one client or one source of traffic.

Anyway, even though my 'side business' was starting to make a small amount of traction, now was really time to make things happen. I hadn't 'loved' this job but I didn't expect to get made redundant from it, and especially in such an abrupt manner.

Isn't it interesting how when your feet are held to the fire things get done? Like the day before you go on holiday, I probably get about 3 times the amount done than on a normal workday. The saying goes that 'it takes pressure to make a diamond, never forget they are not formed overnight' ... well, this really rang true to me here.

I had to figure out a way to generate revenue and fast. Time was against me and I had bills to pay. I actually found another job temporarily - but soon after starting, I was told I might be made redundant again!

As luck had it, I had been branding myself on social media (mostly to look for other jobs) pretty much by accident. Whilst being active on social media, a few people had approached me about consulting them on social media and digital marketing in general. I wasn't convinced at the time, so I tried different business models such as network marketing, but in that industry, nothing really took off for me. So, the most natural route was to go where the market most desired my attention.

Previously, having had a full-time job giving security and comfort, I hadn't been motivated enough to go full time with social media and digital marketing. I guess that is the 'corporate trap' though, isn't it? In fact, my employers were even against me starting my own business, saying this had to be declared and agreed on before it even happened...

After my wakeup call, I decided to take my little 'side hobby' to the next level. Once I started taking things more seriously, my client base started to grow and, because I was doing a good job, word of mouth kicked in with referrals to other businesses.

This was great, but different businesses had different needs, which meant that I needed to expand my knowledge about other digital marketing strategies. I bought courses and went to seminars about email marketing, SEO, YouTube, Facebook advertising, funnels, WordPress, to name but a few.

And I learnt a huge amount, enough to do it for other people full time including selling some of my own offers too. Finally, I didn't need to worry about paying my bills and I didn't need to rely on a full-time traditional job anymore!

Problem is I landed myself in £23K of credit card debt in the process! I always said I'd never buy what I couldn't afford but my hunger to learn and succeed threw all logic out of the window. I don't recommend that you do this by the way, as the majority of these purchases did not get me many results. Mainly because I didn't have the right mindset or commitment level at the time. Also, there were some courses or programmes I bought that were a total waste of money and time.

When it comes to getting started in the consulting world, there should be an easier way to start a consulting business and get clients, without having to spend such money as I did. I believe almost everyone can package and sell their knowledge, as we all have experience others would love to learn from to create a shortcut for them.

You don't have to buy every book, course, mentoring package or offer you come across to be successful. You just need to follow a simple system consistently to have the best chance. Information overload will just hold you back, especially if you go into huge amounts of debt to gain it. It is what you use daily that counts.

For those of you wondering what I do now, I also have digital products and courses where business owners from beginner to advanced skill sets can learn more about how to start getting more qualified leads online, and scale or automate their businesses faster than before. I also run consulting and mentoring programmes if you want to work closer with me in a group, on a real time setting.

I can also provide a 'Done For You' service for the right kind of person, where my team and I create and manage the whole digital marketing process, giving you a hands-free and zero stress way to become an authority online.

That's all well and good but my passion is giving business owners a lifeline to increase leads and revenue. Often that comes from simplifying their business whilst continuing to increase profit generating activities. Basically, my #1 goal is to allow entrepreneurs to fall in love with their business again! If you're a stressed-out business owner working every hour under the sun and more, you know what I mean. Maybe you started a business and now the business is running your life, you feel like you can't take time off. It can be a huge amount of pressure, and if you're not seeing the rewards you deserve it can be hard to stay motivated.

Luckily, social media is a gateway to freedom as it gives you a chance to build an engaged audience. Why is that important? If you have an engaged audience that wants what you're offering, your business is no longer facing a huge issue. That issue being lack of leads or potential buyers.

Later on, in the book I'll touch on marketing strategies that can be combined with social media, to improve your overall marketing efforts. Even though social media is powerful it's still only one strategy, and once you master it you should look to master other strategies too.

It's time to dive into what you should be posting on social media and the best way to get started. There is a lot to take in across the next few chapters, but it's important you understand the whole picture. Let's get started

CHAPTER 4.

WHAT CAN SOCIAL MARKETING SUCCESS DO FOR YOU?

If you're reading this book there's a good chance you have tried to use social media for business before and didn't get any new leads, customers, or sales.

Or you've never used social media to promote your business and aren't sure where to start.

By the time you read this entire book, you'll be able to understand how to not only get results using social media, but in the most time efficient way.

You don't need to spend hours on social media to use it successfully, this is nothing but an urban myth. By now you've probably guessed that scrolling down your news feed for a long time liking random posts doesn't accomplish much apart from a sore thumb, and a feeling of guilt. Like with anything, strategy is key.

Maybe you've seen leaders in your industry easily getting engagement with their huge followings. Perhaps it seems like a constant uphill struggle to build and maintain an audience online, plus turn them into customers.

Or you've been fed strategies by 'gurus' that just aren't cutting it and you want to do something different. Trust me there are a lot of them out there who don't practice what they preach. A lot of them share the bare minimum in their courses and ask you to buy the next course just to get anything useful out of them!

If that's the case, don't worry the best strategies I know of will all be covered in the book. We're going to direct your focus to getting two things from social media - more leads and more customers (or clients). Whilst engagement such as likes and comments on your content is important, it's not going to pay the bills.

I'm also going to share my exact four-step proven system to increase exposure for your business and brand. It's what has allowed me to become a full-time online marketer and something I use all the time, not something I'm preaching that worked years ago.

At one point I never thought I would become highly savvy at using social media, let alone consulting other businesses on how to use it. That said, I don't consider myself an 'expert' or a 'guru' as I'm still learning new things every day. However, after around 4 years of marketing on social media, you do gain some experience of what works and what doesn't.

Want to know something interesting? The job 'Social Media Manager' barely existed 10 years ago, let alone was widely accepted as a standard marketing role within an organisation. Nowadays, even small and medium-sized enterprises (SMEs) are recruiting for talent that relates to knowing how to use social media. Simply type 'social media' into any job site and you will find thousands of related jobs.

Just look at how many results come up on Monster.co.uk alone:

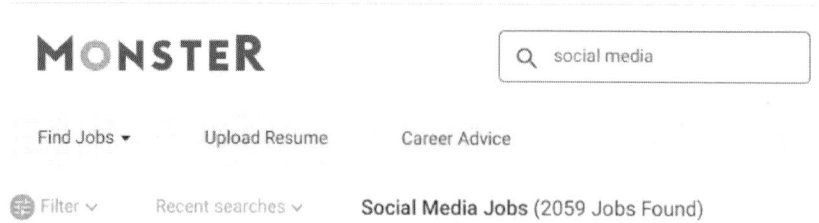

Some are posting that they would like immediate starters which tells you how much demand there is for social media posters and content creators. It's becoming a standard like other traditional roles in an organisation, such as salespeople, bookkeepers, or project managers. You may not be at all interested in a job as a social media manager, but it's a very popular industry for a reason. If you do want a job in social media, you're in luck but there is a lot more competition today than there was even a few years ago.

Never has it been more important to learn a skill like social media, allowing you to present what your business offers in a way that adds value to your audience, whilst also adding value to your bottom line.

Best of all, any business has a chance and you don't need to be highly technical or have a big start up budget to begin.

Social media allows you to get seen so easily. It was the perfect medium for me, a once very shy and insecure person that wouldn't say boo to a goose. I'm less shy and a lot more 'business minded' than when I first started, although my personality hasn't changed entirely. The business world, well that's one of the things it does to you...

Without social media I honestly don't think I would have been able to build a successful business nearly as quickly. Whenever I tried to build a business without it, I always failed and faced rejection. It was one step forward and two backwards the whole time. My background is in systems and processes - so that's what I'm best at - rather than selling or prospecting.

It goes without saying, of course, that a lot of hard work went into using social media to create results. That said, to set the right expectations, social media is not some magic bullet that will triple your business revenue overnight.

It's a tool, just like anything else, and like all tools if not used properly or at all, won't help you. In fact, it could actually damage your business. Using social media will make promoting your business easier, but it still shouldn't be looked at as a shortcut. Like anything there is no guarantee, and it will work for some business models better than others.

I'll share some interesting examples later from some of the biggest companies in the world that cost them some reputation, as well as millions of pounds in market decline and stock prices.

Who is this book for?

This book is primarily for existing business owners; I specifically work with service-based business owners such as coaches, consultants, agency owners, info marketers and anything in between.

My passion is to help them to grow their digital marketing efforts, simplify their online marketing processes, e.g. using automation services, and how to turn their audience into long term satisfied customers.

Even if you aren't an established business that has at least a reasonable budget for marketing and advertising, such as a startup, then you can still benefit from the strategies in this book.

Also, if you don't have a business don't put this book down straight away. If you are looking to start a business of some kind, or even promote a project such as a festival or event, then keep reading as the lessons learned will help you to get these seen by the right people online.

To be blunt, this book is really for anyone sick and tired of seeing others have success with social media and not knowing how to do it for themselves. Even though I typically work with service-based businesses, a lot of this information can be used by product based or traditional businesses. You could be a musician, sell t-shirts or make bespoke desks. I can't really think of a business or trade you may be in that won't benefit at all from what's in this book.

Just be aware that not all the strategies will apply in the exact same way and will vary between industries. You will of course need to get creative and adapt the information to your specific business model to get results. There may be some parts to this book that just don't apply to your industry or business model, and that's fine.

I wanted to make one thing clear about this book before we get going - this isn't going to be a detailed and complex how-to guide for using social media. There are countless tutorials on how to set up things like Facebook profiles and pages already. I didn't write this book to give you brain overload or to bore you with technical information. Plus, by the time I publish this book the information would already be out of date, as these platforms are constantly changing their layout all the time. Often without telling you, giving you quite a shock when you log in and everything has moved!

Instead, I'm going to share concepts and strategies which will be much more valuable for your business. I'm a fairly technical person, but even if you're not the technical side is easy to get past on social media. In fact, knowing the technical side alone won't get you any results at all, you need to know the concepts to make it work.

I've picked the simplest social media site (Facebook) to talk about in this book, so you should be able to get started there without running into many issues. Some of these concepts also go wider than social media and digital marketing. You may find that some of the strategies in the book benefit your business overall. That's no guarantee, but I am fairly confident this will be the case.

The technical side is easy, as you don't need to be building websites or doing anything advanced when you first start. (If you get really stuck you can of course hire someone to do this -for more information check the Resources section towards the end of the book.)

Yes, eventually you will need more digital assets to help to scale up your business, but that isn't the focus of this book. Worrying about these too early on is just creating problems that don't exist yet, and I want you to keep it simple. Sometimes the simplest solutions are the most effective. Let's face it, life is complicated enough isn't it? I hope you'll agree with me that we should keep things simple as much as possible, so long as they get results.

That is the main goal of this book; to help you to gain more exposure, leading to increased leads, clients, or sales, without any complex strategies. Once you start getting results then by all means expand to new territories, but you can't chase two rabbits and catch both of them.

For example, I'm now branching out into other digital marketing strategies - such as email marketing, text message promotion and using webinars. I didn't start out trying to use multiple platforms though. Trying to do all of these on day one would have been a strong recipe for failure, however over time you will want to revisit your strategies and diversify. In the online world things can change very rapidly and it's important to always be testing new ways to market your business.

It's exactly the same for a seasoned investor, would they ever just buy one type of stock or buy just one commodity? Absolutely not - imagine suggesting that to one of the World's top investors, Warren Buffet, and seeing if he keeps a straight face.

Finally, I will mainly be talking about Facebook in this book however these strategies can be used on any platform. You will see me touching on other platforms too as they are better for certain types of content and topics. Later on, in the book I'll explain this more as I go into the different platforms you can use. Let's start with the simplest one that is going to get you set up and build an audience the quickest.

CHAPTER 5.

THE OLD AND THE NEW

Picture this: you are now getting leads, customers and sales from your social media efforts - all for only less than an hour's work per day. Also, I want you to imagine that you are getting potential clients reaching out to you, already wanting to work with you. Meaning that they already know who you are and trust you.

Often you don't even know who the potential client is! They are reaching out to you under the principle of something called 'Attraction Marketing', and although it won't happen every day (especially when you first start), as you build your brand and reputation this becomes increasingly common.

The beauty of this is that as you grow an audience your exposure grows alongside. You'll soon be able to post a status update and have your message seen quickly by a lot more people than trying to advertise to each one by one. After time, engagement will come easily as you'll have a responsive audience keen to know your next move.

On that subject, the ability to use social media the right way lets you use what is called the 'one to many' model. Your business won't be able to grow and scale fast enough unless you increase your exposure. Posting content is how you reach multiple people, instead of trying to get through everybody one by one. It's a pretty simple equation; the more good quality people you can reach about your business, the more likely you are to get leads and customers. Will it happen on day one? It's possible but quite unlikely. Luckily with the strategies I teach, you don't need to invest hours every day into using social media. You can log on, create content, post it and you're pretty much done, aside from interacting with your audience.

In fact, you're not only building your audience but you're also building a digital asset that is valuable to others, not just you. Others may want to advertise on your social media channels if you're perceived to have a responsive audience. If the only asset you have is a 'starving crowd' as an audience, that has a problem you can solve, then your business will likely succeed if you give them what they want.

So just how much is a social media audience worth?

Why don't we put something into perspective and look at how much a single social media post is worth?

If you're a celebrity like Kim Kardashian then you could get paid $300,000 to $500,000 for a single Instagram post*. She probably wouldn't even have to write it and one of her staff would post it.

*Source: Business Insider –

https://www.businessinsider.com/how-much-kim-kardashian-charges-for-instagram-endorsement-deals-2019-5?r=US&IR=T

Love her or hate her, she has a huge following and even if you don't aspire to be like her, you can learn a lot from someone with a following like that. You have to look at successful people and ask yourself "how did they become successful?" whilst putting your thoughts about them aside.

Is she the best entrepreneur or delivering the best quality content? Or is she even the most talented celebrity? Arguably not, although she is still very popular and has a highly valuable digital asset. Valuable enough to the point where you could buy a spacious, newly built 3-bedroom house in my area for the fee Mrs Kardashian is asking for one post! There are way more talented entrepreneurs with a lot more value to give and yet they don't get paid a penny from their posts. Some of them would be lucky to get a thumbs up!

It's exactly the same case with retired wrestler and famous actor Dwayne 'The Rock' Johnson. He charges $1,000,000 to studios if they want him to send a Tweet about the film he is in.*

So why is this the case? Before you start revolting, there is a valid reason and one that you can capitalise on too.

It's because they are entertainers. The world - whether it's right or not - pays a lot more attention to entertainment than to education. That's why TV talk show hosts and comedians like Conan O'Brien or Jimmy Kimmel get paid millions per year. Not only that, but they have a huge amount of influence. I know a business owner that has had a huge amount of backlash from a celebrity using their platform to openly criticise them. It really is having power, and like most powers they can be used for good or bad.

You don't have to be funnier than Conan or Jimmy to get seen and heard on social media, but you do have to be somewhat entertaining. You also have to give some great insight in your content and combine it with entertainment. Think of how you can provide 'infotainment' and your audience will be hanging on your every word. Otherwise over time you will definitely lose your audience to someone more interesting - sorry, I said it!

So now the next step is turning engagement into leads and customers for your sales. Don't worry, you don't need to have millions of followers to do this, not even close.

If you have more leads than you know what to do with, you're in a winning position. That is exactly what we are going to figure out for you. Not just get likes, comments and shares, but create actual conversations with potential clients or customers.

The best part of this, is that you can do this all on a bootstrap style budget. Gone are the days that you need a corporate sized amount of cash to advertise. Virtually any business can get set up to use social media for free, starting from today.

*Source: Vulture - 'The Rock Charges Studios $1 Million If They Want Him to Tweet About the Movie He's In'. Retrieved from https://www.vulture.com/2018/05/the-rock-is-charging-million-dollars-to-promote-his-next-movie-online.html

CHAPTER 6.

WHAT YOU SHOULD BE POSTING

Why do so many people struggle to succeed on social media?

This is a question I hear often, and of course you could argue there are all kinds of reasons. Some might say it's because of too much competition, turbulent market conditions, or even having your social media account shut down!

In my opinion, the biggest reason is that people over complicate the process in terms of what content to post, to the point where they don't ever take enough or any action. One thing I love about social media is that the algorithms which run the platforms will punish you if you're not using the platform correctly. For example, if you're being overly promotional and not engaging with your audience.

Just so I'm clear, you shouldn't be using social media to spam your business, products, or service. By spamming I mean just posting your links or offers to your business - as if you're putting up flyers at bus stops. Nobody logs onto social media with their credit card in hand, they need to know, like and trust you before they buy first. Also, people are at different stages of buying, although that could be a book in itself...

So, the question is, how do you use social media to get exposure for your business? What are the exact steps you need to take to achieve this?

You shouldn't just have an online profile on these sites and do nothing with them. Your next step is to create something called content.

Content is an online post of some kind on any online platform, such as an image posted on Facebook or an article on your blog.

There are many different forms of content but here are the key types you need to be aware of:

Text Posts

These are simple text-only posts, without any images or videos. Some would say they are too boring, but they can still capture attention if crafted properly. They are quick and easy to do, so if you're in a hurry they're ideal and of course much better than nothing. Here is an example:

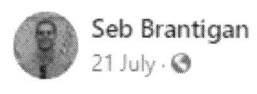

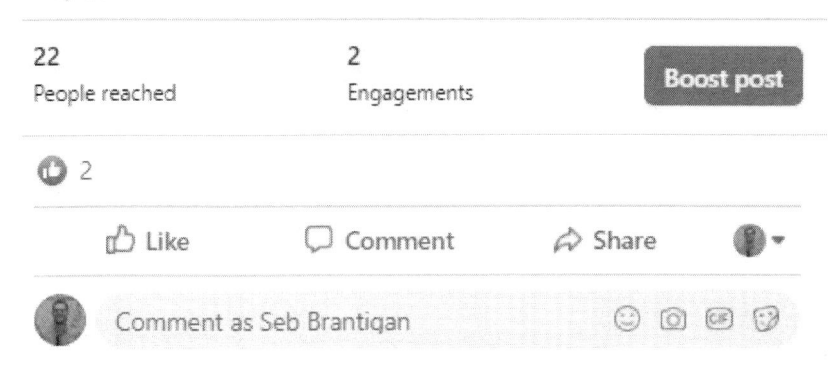

> **Seb Brantigan**
> 21 July
>
> Never underestimate the power of CONTRAST in your marketing. Meaning, making something stand out or look different...it goes a long way 👀
>
> | 22 | 2 | |
> |---|---|---|
> | People reached | Engagements | Boost post |
>
> 👍 2
>
> 👍 Like   💬 Comment   ↗ Share
>
> Comment as Seb Brantigan

Images

Images can be posted on their own or with some text. No, I'm not just talking about constantly taking 'selfies' or pictures of your dog! Good image posts should be colourful, high quality and easy to read on all devices. Most platforms like Facebook will automatically optimise images so advanced editing isn't often needed, but you will want to make sure any text inside images isn't too small.

Here is an example:

Seb Brantigan
2 March

While I'm a very positive person online and in real life I'm far from perfect and have my flaws.

I'm quite reserved and if I do go occasionally go to social or networking events, sometimes I struggle to talk to people. Often times I talk myself out of going and buy my own excuses easily

In the past I've been too nice and offered too much to the point it put me at my own detriment.... See more

Videos (Pre-Recorded)

They say a picture is 1000 words, if that's the case then 1000 pictures must make a video. A good video will be produced in landscape mode (to avoid the dreaded 'black bars' surrounding it), concise, and without lots of background noise.

You might want to consider getting a good microphone as poor sound is harder to hide than poor quality video. You may or may not agree with me on this, but there's nothing more distracting than background noise in a video and it's hard to concentrate on the actual message. That said, lighting is very important so recording videos during the day is recommended. My best tip is to look into the camera lens when recording a video, if you can. Always consider the user experience and make it easy for them to see and hear your content. Here is an example:

Seb Brantigan
1 February

So you've started your business as a consultant, coach, freelancer etc. However getting enough people to look at your business is an uphill struggle. You just can't fill the pipeline quick enough.

In this video is my recommendation about what to do if you're stuck.

Join the Facebook group Unstoppable Marketing Public Group - Seb Brantigan

252
People reached

10
Engagements

Boost post

Yep, I picked the video where I look like I'm about to sneeze! Don't worry you can change what is called the Thumbnail in the video settings after you publish it.

Side note here, as above you will also see a 'Boost Post' button which is related to paid advertising - I tend to ignore this and carry on with my day. More on this in later chapters.

Videos (Live)

See the above explanation for videos, but these are live broadcasts! Live videos are less common because very few people actually do these, let alone videos at all. So, if you're super confident talking about your business, then doing live videos will definitely place you miles ahead of your competition.

The downside to doing live videos is that you need above average Internet. From experience, even a slight dip in Internet speed can make your live streams difficult for the viewer to video properly and your live stream might end abruptly. Also, the overall quality isn't as good as a pre-recorded video.

Here is an example, although they appear more or less the same as a pre-recorded video on your audience's newsfeed:

How do you get GREAT
testimonials even if you don't ha...
45 weeks ago · 3.5K views

2

Articles

Articles are longer text posts that are usually at least a few hundred words, they may also contain images or videos. Many content sites have a separate section entirely to create articles which let you add in more media. This in itself is a downside as they don't usually show in people's newsfeeds, although you can easily share a link to the article with your audience.

LinkedIn is a great place to post and read articles or blog posts, they seem to be very avid readers there. Platforms like Facebook don't have many articles posted onto the platform whereas you will see this more on LinkedIn.

Depending on your market and if you're a dab hand at writing (or at least enjoy it) you may want to write articles as a way to gain exposure.

Here's an example on LinkedIn:

Not sure what to say?

Published on December 29, 2019 | Edit article | View stats

Seb Brantigan
Digital Marketing Growth Consultant at Brantigan Enterprises LTD

2 articles

If you get tongue-tied when it comes to creating content or writing emails, let these few lessons be a warm helping hand...

Once you know your market deep-down to the core, such as what keeps them up at night, what they worry about in general, but also what appeals to them...you've done the hard work.

When it comes to choosing whether to do text-posts, images, or videos it depends on which you enjoy doing the most. You might love typing or writing but are camera shy, in which case articles are likely the best option for you. Or if you're a natural on camera then start with video. It helps to vary types of content but stick with the one you would be happy to do every day.

Some topics you can post text-posts, images, and videos about:

- News/Current Affairs
- Case Studies/Testimonials
- Trivia/Polls
- Inspirational
- Informative, e.g. 3 tips to XYZ
- Personal Stories

One tip I can give you is that if you are posting any links along with your content, be sure to put these into the comments section of your post AFTER you hit publish. Social media platforms like Facebook will show your posts to less people if they have links in them that take you away from the platform.

I wanted to show you the difference between a Facebook Business Page and a Facebook Group as I have experienced some confusion amongst users.

Facebook Business Page - this is different to your own page (known as a Personal Page). A Business Page acts similar to a website, as you can add details about your business or brand - such as opening hours, mission statements etc. Your clients and customers can post reviews there too. You will find lots of options to add information about your business, to the point that at the start some businesses may not even require a detailed website.

Here's an example of a Facebook Business Page (the layout will look different on mobile devices):

Facebook Group

Below you will see that this looks similar to a Business Page, but there is more interaction that happens here. A Facebook Group page acts more like an Internet forum than a website. And worth noting that you can't pay to advertise from a Group.

Here's an example of a Facebook Group belonging to one of my clients:

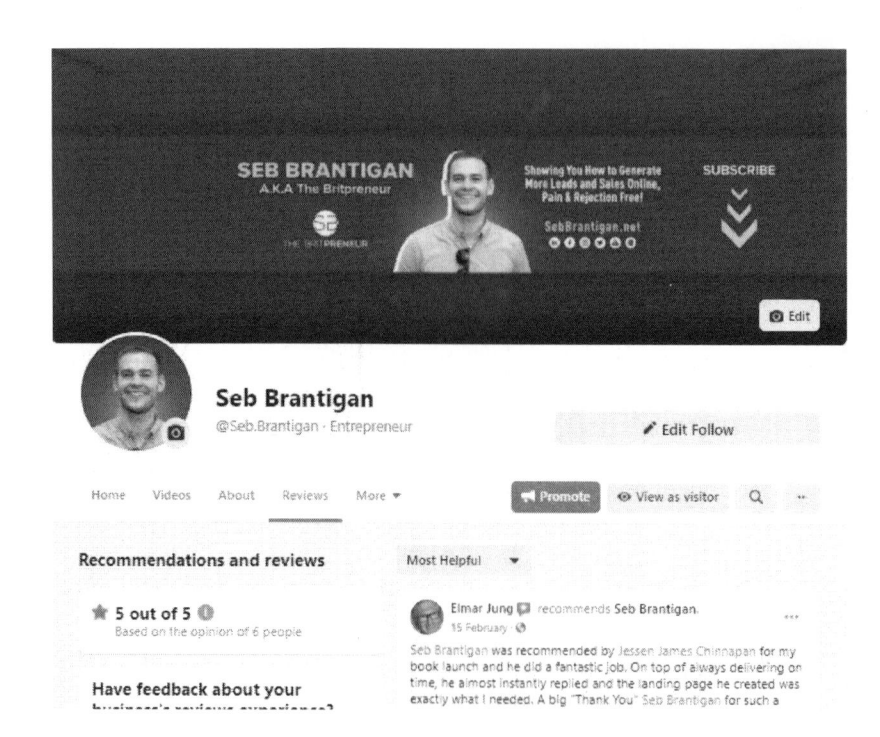

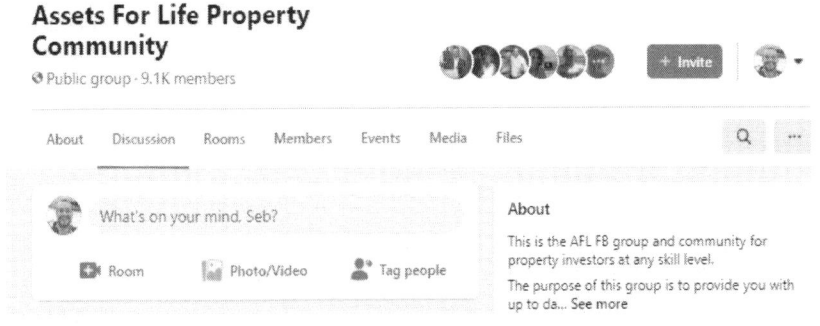

Out of both Pages and Groups, I would say that Groups are the best places to find your ideal target market, where it's easiest to interact with people.

As an example, to find marketing related Groups, you can use the search bar and type in 'marketing' as per below (this also works for Pages):

🅕 🔍 marketing

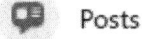

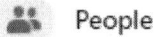

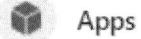

Search results for
marketing

Filters

- 🗔 All
- 💬 Posts
- 👥 People
- 🖼 Photos
- ▶ Videos
- 🏬 Marketplace
- 🚩 Pages
- 📍 Places
- 👥 Groups
- 📦 Apps

This is where you can find endless people to talk to about a topic relating to your business. Looking to find stay at home Mums or Dads? Need to talk to Property Developers? How about those into gardening and home improvement? There are Groups and Pages dedicated to all of these causes and more. Just one Group could have hundreds of thousands of your ideal clients inside, so it's well worth using them to get exposure to your business.

Another great thing you can do with Pages, is to watch the type of content your competitors post on theirs. See who the most influential or popular business or icon is in your industry and see if they are posting content that gets great engagement. If the content is popular, you have an idea of what kind of content your particular market likes to see. Nope, you really don't need to reinvent the wheel!

Just make sure that if you interact on Pages and Groups that you follow the theme of this book, and just post great quality content. Your intention is to network and get to know people in the group. Just like at a networking event, if you keep showing up and sharing some useful insight without pitching, people will begin to gravitate towards you. Don't start posting links to your business or blatantly advertising, you'll run the risk of getting banned from these places before you even know it.

While this is all well and good, how can you turn engagement on social media into leads and customers for your business?

Now that is the million-pound question...

Getting people to like, comment and share your content is one thing. Sparking up a conversation with them is another!

This is where a LOT of people miss the mark and get it wrong. They think that they can build a business without actually having a conversation with people. At some point this will definitely be necessary, especially if you have a higher priced product. People simply won't buy from people they don't trust.

It's possible to spend all day on social media trying to engage and interact with people, without actually growing your business. Instead, you need to have a real conversation with people that doesn't include a few comments here and there in a status post.

The easiest way to do this, is to simply start a conversation with someone who has recently interacted with one of your statuses. It's surprising how few people do this, when the reality is some of these people would be keen to talk to you.

You never know if someone is secretly looking to work with you but is too shy to pipe up about it. Very few people will take the time to contact someone by directly messaging them and yet it doesn't take long to do. Yes, it still happens from time to time, but you won't get floods of people beating down your door to buy your offer. If it were that easy, you wouldn't be reading a book on how to get customers! Just start a conversation without having "I need to make a sale!" in your head, and you will be surprised how receptive people are. Even over the Internet people can still tell if you're being pushy or desperate for a sale, so it just isn't worth going for it too early. Focus on relationship building and creating the engaged audience first. There will come a time when you can talk about what you do, but relationships always come first. Often enough if you are posting regular valuable content, people will ask you first about your business. That is when Attraction Marketing starts to fall into place, and you get people chasing you about your business.

That's exactly why you need to not only stay consistent with posting content, but also 'bite the bullet' and reach out to those who interact with you. Initially, if you're not well known in your space, people won't automatically reach out to you. It could take years for this to happen, so it's not something you should expect soon after posting content. Once you grow your brand however, this will start to happen more and more.

You've probably heard the phrase 'the fortune is in the follow up'. Social media is a great way of people seeing your message and brand on a regular basis. It's an indirect follow up as you don't have to physically speak to them.

That said, if you are selling a product that is expensive (a top tier product) or a service that is quite technical, it may be difficult to sell online. Certain offers require a conversation over the phone or video chat. Platforms such as Facebook make this very easy as you can phone or video call via their Messenger app for free, using your mobile data or WiFi (also known as Voice Over Internet Protocol - basically calling others online).

Just how powerful are online calls and video chats?

Facebook bought WhatsApp Inc in February 2014 for $19.3billion (£14.64bn), another app that lets you phone or video call for free. This feature revolutionised how we communicate. The same can be said for platforms like Zoom, which have features such as recording conversations and remote access.

Texts and phone calls are still being used but for some are no longer a preferred form of communication. For example, I no longer need to worry about racking up a high phone bill to reach my clients in the USA and other parts of the world.

In the next chapter, I will be revealing my four step 'Formula' I have created which is tried, tested and easy to follow.

CHAPTER 7.

AN INTRODUCTION TO THE FOUR STEP FORMULA

Over the years I've done so much trial and error when it comes to online marketing, in particular with social media. If I were to put all of this into a book for you, it would be like another edition of War and Peace! So, I wondered "what if I could share the best ways to get started with social media marketing in a simple way?" as I was learning the best way to go about it myself. After a lot of experience, I've managed to condense it into my four step system.

This is my four-step system to getting more leads, clients, and exposure on social media without any complicated set up. Best of all anyone can use this, and you don't need to be a marketing or technical expert to follow it. It's called:

The Four Step 'P. I. M. P.' Formula

Before I explain what this formula it is, I know it's a bit of a crazy acronym (and hopefully not too offensive). The reason for that is I want you to memorise it and of course, use it. Your brain remembers unusual things, so P. I. M. P. seemed to tick that box.

The Four Step 'P. I. M. P.' Formula stands for:

- Platform
- Identify
- Message
- Promotion

The great thing about this four-step formula is that it will fit perfectly on a post-it note so you can carry this anywhere you go.

In the following chapters I'll be breaking down each of the four steps and how they work, but before we dive in here's a brief explanation of each step.

The Four Step 'P. I. M. P.' Formula

FROM THE BRITPRENEUR

Platform
THE EASY AUDIENCE FINDER PLAN
My exact system to pick the best platform to promote your business on.

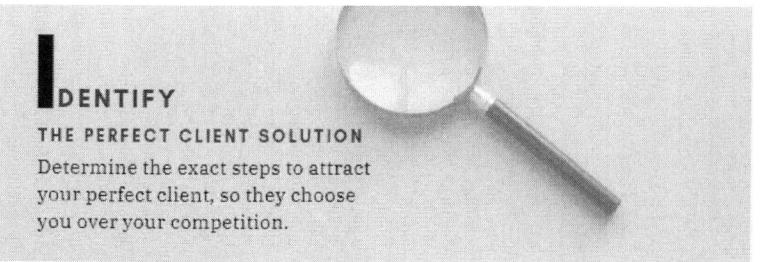

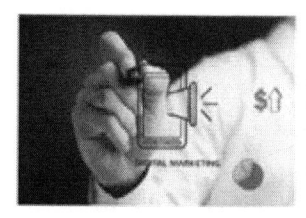

Identify
THE PERFECT CLIENT SOLUTION
Determine the exact steps to attract your perfect client, so they choose you over your competition.

Message
THE MAGENTIC CONTENT FORMULA
Research before writing your copy. Tell your readers how they can benefit from using your product.

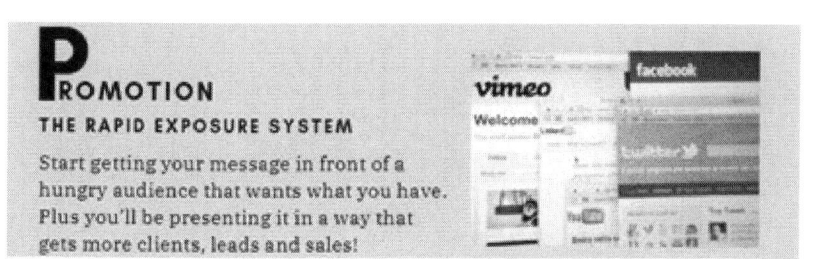

Promotion
THE RAPID EXPOSURE SYSTEM
Start getting your message in front of a hungry audience that wants what you have. Plus you'll be presenting it in a way that gets more clients, leads and sales!

AN INTRODUCTION TO THE FOUR STEP FORMULA

Let's dive into each of these four steps and how you can apply them to your business starting today!

CHAPTER 8.

PLATFORM (THE EASY AUDIENCE FINDER PLAN)

One of the hardest things people struggle with is finding the right platform on which to promote their business. Here are some of the platforms I recommend using:

- Facebook
- YouTube
- LinkedIn

You also have other platforms - which I don't personally use a lot - but are still an option:

- Instagram
- TikTok

- Snapchat
- Reddit
- Twitter
- Pinterest

You could also define Facebook's Messenger and WhatsApp services as social media platforms too.

Now, some businesses work better on other platforms and there are of course hundreds of platforms out there I've not listed. For example, Facebook does not let you advertise certain businesses, as they are against their terms of service.

Instead, other sites such as YouTube are a better platform for certain businesses, especially if you have a product or service that is hard to describe. Depending on your offer, your audience may be easier to reach on YouTube than on Facebook.

LinkedIn is more business focused than other platforms, so if you are doing B2B you may wish to start there. If you don't wish to use Facebook's platform to market your business, that's fine as there are so many out there. You can just take what you've learnt and adapt it elsewhere.

If in doubt, I recommend testing each platform until you decide which you prefer using. If you don't find a platform easy to use, the chances are you won't have much success with it, and you might find it a chore. That said you still need to pick one platform and run with whichever you like best.

Once you master one platform, you can begin working on building an audience on a new one. When you're first getting started I don't recommend using more than two platforms at any one time, unless you have someone helping you with the content creation or management.

Be aware that each of these platforms have their own algorithms to work with. The definition of an algorithm is 'a process or set of rules to be followed in calculations or other problem-solving operations, especially by a computer'*. These algorithms determine which pieces of content show up in peoples' newsfeeds, where they show up or even prevent content showing up at all.

*Source: Oxford Languages, Google.com

CHAPTER 9.

IDENTIFY (THE PERFECT CLIENT SOLUTION)

Before jumping the gun and getting content created, you need to decide who your content is going to be aimed at. You need to be clear on who they are, as well as who they aren't (you can come back to who to exclude later).

Here is a non-exhaustive list of demographic related questions that can help you to decide on your targeting:

- How old is this person?
- Are they male or female?
- Are they single, married, divorced, or in a civil partnership?

- What is their income level?
- Did they go to University?

It doesn't just stop at demographics, that's just the beginning. Here is another list of questions that make you think about the daily problems they experience.

- What pisses them off?
- What are they most afraid of?
- What keeps them up at night?
- What are their political views?
- Do they hate their boss or career?
- What are their goals and aspirations?
- What motivates them to get up every day?
- What do their spending habits say about them?
- What do they do to relax and how often does this happen?
- What is something negative in their life that they'd like to change?
- Are they facing any kind of transition in life, such as moving cities, starting a new job or a relationship change?

If you have completed this exercise before, you may have heard the term 'Avatar' (derived from the film) which is the process I'm talking about here.

A great piece of homework I'm going to give you, is to map out who this perfect client is, as if they are a real person. Use the above questions to guide you.

You can even give them a full name, political view and favourite food if you so wish. The more detailed the better, as you can make your message more specific.

Then, imagine you are going for a drink with them or out for dinner and are getting to know them. Think about the types of responses they would give to your questions.

At first it might feel like you're signaling people out and you won't get the volume of people you want, because you're being too specific. The truth is if you're targeting everyone then you really end up targeting no-one.

"My product or service is for anyone!", is a typical response I hear a lot from someone who hasn't been through this process. Why is the Identify step so important? It means you can target who would be most likely to buy your product. Ideally people that are already buying something similar to what you're selling.

For example, if you sell health vitamins you would be best to market these to those who are into health and wellness - such as personal trainers. Just look at your competition to see what kind of customers they have.

It is possible to have more than one key audience that you are targeting, but to avoid watering down your message too much I would stick to a maximum of two audiences. For example, if you are a business coach, your audience could be existing business owners and someone who has just started a business. We all know that are certain types of people more likely to buy than others, so we should target them as a priority.

You can look on Facebook pages, inside Groups, online forums and many more places to find such people. This research aspect is so important - I advise spending at least half a day on the Identify step alone. Consider the famous quote "give me six hours to chop down a tree and I will spend the first four sharpening the axe" by Abraham Lincoln. It's exactly the same when it comes to any marketing campaign, not just social media. For long term marketing campaigns, it wouldn't be unusual for me to spend several days mapping out the Identity of the potential customers. So, don't rush this step because it could make or break your business.

There is also a way you can target your competition to legitimately 'steal' their customers using paid advertising. Yes, your competition can actually help you to grow your business without knowing it! I'll get into that in more detail more later in the book.

My best advice is to not move forward until you are super clear on your Avatar - not doing this could make the rest of the process pointless. The content you post will get minimal engagement, if any. It would be like selling steak to vegans. If in doubt, do some more research until you're absolutely sure you know who your Avatar is.

This might change as you start to put content out into the marketplace and different audiences start to take an interest in your product or service. Ultimately your goal is to find more customers and clients on social media, so it's important to know which kind of content is achieving this. Make a start and get clear on day one to ensure you get the most out of your marketing efforts.

CHAPTER 10.

MESSAGE - (THE MAGNETIC CONTENT FORMULA)

Once you know who your content is aimed at, the next step is to create content specific for this audience. In this part of the process, you will want to decide on your medium of content (video, text) and a good idea when creating content is to start it with a question.

Here's a few examples you can adapt:

"Are you a business consultant that is managing to get clients but they're not the clients you want?"

"Is your business making money but not making a profit?"

"Do you spend more time managing staff and processes than actually doing what you love in your business?"

"As a business owner do you feel like you've been promised a dream but are living a nightmare?"

This is why the Identify step is crucial here, as what this does is it speaks to the audience you want to target. If needs be, go back and spend at least a few hours on it as it will make this step much easier.

One way to break this down further is to pinpoint who you are aiming the message at (business owner), paint a picture for them (they have a great service) but then hit them with a pain point they're experiencing (lack of customers). The more you can relate to them and speak their language, the more your audience will engage with it. You should focus on content that they would find useful and can't get enough of.

Imagine social media as if it were a traditional business that relied on footfall. You probably would only want people to go inside your business that would be interested in your offer. Anybody else would not only be wasting your time but would be taking up space for someone who is genuinely interested. You could be losing a lot of money by inviting the wrong people into your business.

By posting the wrong Message you will only invite the wrong people, who won't interact with your content or become a customer. You will basically spin your wheels and be creating content that nobody cares about.

Now that's not to say that you should only be posting content about your business all of the time. Even if your industry is quite a 'highbrow' serious type of industry that isn't based on entertainment, there's no reason why you can't talk about personal achievements, family, friends and even your favourite sport.

Any time that your engagement tends to 'dip' is a good opportunity to stop talking about anything business related, even though your business will be the main topic of your content. Sometimes you will want to change things up by posting about content that everyone can relate to, such as going out and about and seeing friends or family. Otherwise you risk losing your audience or simply boring them, driving them elsewhere - such as into the arms of your competition.

Remember that a big part of social media is engagement; you want to be talking with people and not just at them. This is why posting links on your profile or Business Page should be done sparingly, unless it's combined with lots of content as mentioned in Chapter 6.

One bonus tip I want to give you to engage people is to tell more stories in your content. People love to read and hear stories, especially when emotion is involved. As the saying goes 'facts tell and stories sell'. If you can weave stories into your content will make it far more interesting than most content other people are posting.

Next is the final step that arguably is the most crucial, which allows you to put the other three steps to the test.

CHAPTER 11.

PROMOTION (THE RAPID EXPOSURE SYSTEM)

This is where the rubber truly hits the road and where all the magic comes together. Following the Rapid Exposure System is basically the process of combining the previous three steps and doing it consistently, with added urgency.

If you're new to social media and don't have much of a following, then you will need to be posting often. Often meaning at least once a day if you are doing this on a part time basis, more than once a day if you are doing this full time. You'll need to stand apart by posting more often than your competitors who post less often (or not at all!). The same applies in sales. Sometimes it is a numbers game, even if you are being strategic you do need volume. If you're in sales and you have mastered a pitch that has a 100% close rate, you will still get zero results if you have no qualified prospects.

In the beginning your goal is still to provide great quality to your audience, but you will need to be extremely proactive. In fact, I would go as far to say there isn't a limit to how much content you should post - there is never 'too much' content that you can get out there, especially in the beginning. Quality should always top quantity, however being seen and heard is a lot more important.

At first it will take time to get engagement on your posts, and you may not see any likes or comments initially for some time. Don't get disheartened; there are times when I've been inboxed by people who have followed my content, but have never engaged with me. In some cases, they know exactly who I am and I don't even know who they are - it gives you a bit of a cool 'celebrity' feeling. This is what is called building authority, and this is a big factor in getting people to buy from you. It does however take time to build that authority and to become well known on social media.

In some cases, these 'strangers' have been potential customers that turned into long term buyers, becoming a client or customer with me for years. So, by not posting and engaging with your audience regularly, you are doing your business a disservice. You just never know who is watching your content but too afraid to engage right away, or some people just prefer not to engage at all.

Think of it like this; the day you stop posting content could be the day a potential customer decides to contact you about buying... but then they forget and get distracted by one of your competitors who is posting more than you.

Look at Coca Cola for example. It's in every shop, bar, hotel, café, you name it, and that's not including their billboards or other advertising. They're an omnipresent brand to the point where it's almost impossible to avoid them. As a result, it's become a household name and for most of us, a first choice for a soft drink anywhere we go.

The harsh reality is you could be leaving untold amounts of money on the table, and all because you didn't take action consistently. The worst part? You might not even know it, giving up right before a long-term customer shows up. I see 'entrepreneurs' throwing in the towel early far too often. In certain business types and models, you only need a few customers per month to be doing well. Sometimes, all it takes is one client or customer to really get the ball rolling.

I am all for posting good quality content, but you need to be doing this as often as possible. Think about McDonald's, they probably don't have the best burger (product) in the world, but they do have great marketing and a proven business model.

It is a predictable experience; every McDonald's I have been to, even outside of the UK is virtually the same (except in Spain where you can enjoy your meal with a beer!), and kids are obsessed with it. Look at the creation of Ronald McDonald and Happy Meals. which makes kids fall in love with the brand. The adults for the most part go along with it, so McDonald's ends up being a family treat. Meaning that parents are pretty much forced to be 'McLoving It' too!

It is the marketing of a product (or service) that will catapult your business to success the fastest. Now that's not to say you can neglect your product quality, you still need a good product or eventually your business will build up quite a bad press. It just doesn't have to be absolutely perfect to the point where you don't get your offer out there.

Many small and medium-sized business owners aren't promoting themselves or their business enough, because they think they need to offer all the bells and whistles. Nope, the truth is that there are businesses out there with a more inferior product or service but are doing very well in the marketplace. All because they put their best foot forward, and although they don't have everything right, they are at least showing up every day. 80% is the new 100%, as one of my mentors says, and overthinking or procrastination (both are similar) are the killer of countless would-be thriving businesses.

When I first launched this book, I was contacting people directly by their inbox to promote it, not in a spammy way or anything. I let them know that I was launching a book and would they be able to support me on the book launch. All I asked for was a yes or no answer, but with the underlying dual purpose to promote the book.

Here's more about sending direct messages which I highly recommend:

The next step of your marketing process - i.e. phone call, consultation - will result from the inboxes of your social media account even though this is where the connections begin. However you need to be careful about inboxing people the right way.

You don't want to be sending people links all the time about your offer, but you can still show your passion about your business without acting like a spammer. Very rarely would I recommend sending any promotional links about your business to someone you've never spoken to before. Links to your blog or other social media channels are fine but you shouldn't send these in the first message. Also, you don't want to be sending out more than 30 or so messages in one day, as the social platforms will think you're spamming. This is especially easier for their systems to detect if you're sending links. You could lose your account by sending too many messages too quickly, so make sure to 'chill' in between sending batches of messages.

Let's get back to talking about promotion as a whole.

So long as your offer solves a problem, your business will succeed if you focus on sales and marketing. No business can grow unless it is consistently getting people through the door every day. Having a compelling and irresistible offer is important, but making sure enough people see that offer is important too.

The last thing I wanted to leave you with in this chapter, is that there are two types of people on social media. Content creators and content consumers. Which of the two do you believe is leading the way? Obviously, the goal is to become a content creator, the minority.

Not all your content will be successful. If you've ever heard of the 80/20 rule, you'll know that in marketing 80% of your results typically come from 20% of your efforts. You just have to keep going and testing new content.

One little 'hack' I can suggest to you is to repost content that gets good engagement - if it's not broken why fix it? Just don't do it right away, be sure to wait at least a few weeks before reposting. You don't always have to post totally unique content every single time. Social media platforms like Facebook will only show your content to the most engaged people in your audience. Not all of your followers will see all of your posts especially if you are competing against many other content creators and adverts, which is why it's important to post so regularly. Especially when it comes to posting on different topics, as different people will find some topics more interesting than others.

I figured some of the readers of this book might be worried about writing the wrong kind of content, so in the next chapter I wanted to include some examples of what to be thinking about when posting content.

CHAPTER 12.

WHAT TO AVOID

Whilst it's important to know what kind of content is worth posting, here's some examples of how *not* to do it. I wanted to give you live examples which were seen by millions of people, and while you most likely don't have an audience that size (yet!), I want to stress the importance of context as well as content.

Not following these rules could leave you vulnerable to what is called 'cancel culture' which is where companies or celebrities get boycotted and publicly shamed. If you're new to social media then your audience might be a bit more forgiving, but it's unlikely.

If you're not sure how social media can actually make your business worse off, you may want to check out these weird and not-so-wonderful posts:

Example 1* -Starbucks

I encourage you to read it over and over - as it makes no sense to me, and to the millions of people that saw it:

INTRODUCING STARBUCKS® BLONDE ESPRESSO

Who says espresso has to be intense?

We have for 43 years.

But we're Starbucks Coffee Company.

So we did the exact opposite.

Example 2* -US Dept of Education*

US Dept of Education ✓
@usedgov

Follow

Education must not simply teach work - it must teach life. – W.E.B. DeBois

3:45 PM - Feb 12, 2017

💬 3,069　↺ 3,597　♡ 5,273

The irony of this one writes itself (the correct spelling is DuBois not DeBois).

While these are relatively harmless examples which might make you smile, unfortunately more ignorant ones have been posted.

*Source for Example 1, 2: impactbnd.com

WHAT TO AVOID

Example 3* -Miele, German manufacturer of appliances

Miele ✓
8 March at 05:30

May all women always remember to embrace what makes them unique!

Happy International Women's Day!

#Miele #MieleUAE #ImmerBesser #ForeverBetter #InternationalWomensDay

www.miele.ae

You can probably guess the reaction from female viewers of this post as it portrays 60's housewife stereotypes more than anything. As you may have guessed it caused some backlash and did not give their loyal followers the intended message.

*Source for Example 3: krusecontrolinc.com

Miele subsequently apologised and have since removed this post, however once something is published there is little you can do to unpublish content (with the exception being if there are legal issues, such as ownership of content being claimed by others). Even though this post was deleted from Miele's social media account quickly, I was still able to find it via an easy Google search.

These content posts aren't fatal however some were quite careless, and more than likely caused some long-term customers to be lost. Not to mention a large loss for the company's stock price if these posts went viral and the media published them. All of them were avoidable and caused a lot of unnecessary stress. Probably something you don't need more of in your business!

To summarise, think hard about what you're posting especially if it's going to be controversial. There is a right and a wrong way to do this, and I'm not saying you can't be controversial. Sometimes that is a great way to get engagement, especially if your brand is new. It just needs some strategy to ensure you're delivering the right message and to protect your brand...as well as not offending too many people of course!

These examples haven't been included here to drive you away from creating content, they're there to encourage you to think *differently* when creating content. The truth is, if you know your audience well, it's unlikely you will be creating content that might offend them. You're more likely to make the odd spelling mistake, which funnily enough by itself can create more engagement by people pointing it out. Yes, you read it here first, making mistakes on social media can actually work in your favour!

If you do post something damaging it can be difficult for your audience to forget it. So, choose your words carefully, as people are more consumer wise than they ever have been. The Internet is written in ink not pencil, so think twice about your message.

That said, we all make mistakes and have said things out loud which we regret later. Social media is no different, so resign to the fact that you will make mistakes. At least you're doing it early on while you're still learning and building an audience. You might even offend people talking about a non-offensive topic. That is the key here though, to pick your topics carefully. However, realise that some people may be offended by what you say, but at the end of the day we're all entitled to our own opinions.

Think about issues people would normally argue over. Politics, religion, war - anything that might cause uproar even at a casual family dinner table. Dividing topics like these should be talked about sparingly, and if being talked about always come from a place of hearing other peoples' thoughts. Just be indifferent and hear people out on their views. It not only helps with your engagement, but it creates a deeper relationship with your audience.

You could definitely open up a debate on these subjects, just don't make it about your opinion - unless you don't mind defending it. If you've ever seen people argue on social media, it can go on and on forever if you let it.

Whilst talking about controversial topics can be great for your engagement, it's not always a positive experience for everyone. If someone sees negative comments on your profile or page and it's the first time they've come across you, they could get the wrong idea if you started the discussion.

You could be starting a war rather than a nice discussion, and things can get out of hand quite quickly. Unfortunately, you simply can't trust that people can give their opinion in a kind and fair way. Also consider that things can be easily misread online which makes arguments more common than you would typically see in real life.

Remember, your objective is to generate exposure via your content that will lead more people to see your business and brand. You definitely don't want to be known for creating controversial topics or content, it certainly won't attract the right people to your business.

Consider that as your reputation grows, you will become more visible and this might attract the wrong people to you by accident. These are the people that lurk on your social media, trying to point out a mistake and make you look bad. You may know these friendly characters as 'trolls' who will jump at the opportunity to twist your words. These personalities will likely show up even on status posts with a more positive spin to them, however controversial topics are more likely to catch their eye.

Be aware that if they show up, they will try to get others to 'side' with them against you. In this instance the best thing to do is to stand your ground, remaining professional. Obviously, if someone is just being a bit brutal and has nothing constructive to offer, you should delete their comments and block them. The last thing you want to do is to start an endless 'Internet war' with a troll who can beat you at their own game. Or to leave a trail of negativity which just inspires more negativity. With the slightly less abrasive trolls, try to have some fun with them if you can. It helps your engagement - let the trolls lend a hand in trying to build your business without them even knowing it!

Lastly, you should avoid the temptation of buying followers, friends, fans, or anything inauthentic and fake. It might make you look good to some people, but most will see right through it, as you won't have much engagement. You can also buy engagement in a legitimate way, such as advertising on Facebook to get more likes on your Business Page. That is the only exception and doing anything else could also put your account at risk. Most social media platforms could ban you forever for doing so. It's just not worth it and if someone finds out it would give you a bad reputation. Plus, you aren't buying engagement that will lead to any actual results. This makes it harder to figure out who the genuine people are that engage with your content.

CHAPTER 13.

WHAT IT TAKES TO GO VIRAL

While you don't need your content to get millions of views to start getting leads, it helps to know what kind of content can be popular to post. In a lot of cases, it's not something that can be repeated easily, and it is largely down to luck. It can be as simple as a celebrity sharing a content post at random, to their audience of millions just because it particularly resonates with them.

Often, it comes down to the right message being in front of the right people at the right time. Even though your content most likely won't circle round the globe anytime soon, studying why viral posts go viral is still useful.

Example A

Here's the story about the egg that cracked the Instagram record for the most liked picture. A picture of an egg was posted to the platform on 4 January 2019. Why? It was in response to Kylie Jenner's photo of her daughter, which at the time was the most liked post on Instagram.

Image Source: Instagram.com

To date it has 54.4 million likes and is still the most liked picture on Instagram. Perhaps you could say they cracked the code to get the most engagement?

My poor jokes aside, here's why this story is relevant; content creation doesn't always have to be complicated. The picture of an egg was simple, but it had a mission and story behind it, and that's why it went viral.

In fact, sometimes the simpler your content is and easier it is for people to understand its message, the better. If you're new to content creation, don't focus so much on writing long and complex pieces of content.

Doing so can make it easy to dilute your message and giving yourself a mission to write long pieces of content can be a good reason to procrastinate the task.

Example B)

The hashtag #Movember.

Men's mental health has become a popular topic in recent years especially with men aged 45-49 having the highest rate of suicides, according to Samaritans.org. Movember describe themselves as 'the leading global organisation committed to changing the face of men's health'.

The use of this hashtag has helped to quickly spread awareness of both the charity and the cause across the world. There were even razor brands such as Billie encouraging women to get involved.

> **veronica** @veronica_v18 · 30 Oct
> Ladies, throw your razors away this month as we are encourage to participate in #Movember and celebrate the fact that "women have moustaches too" #comm220smmnews **Billie's** New Campaign Is the First Women's Razor Ad to Show Facial Hair glamour.com/story/billie-m... via @glamourmag

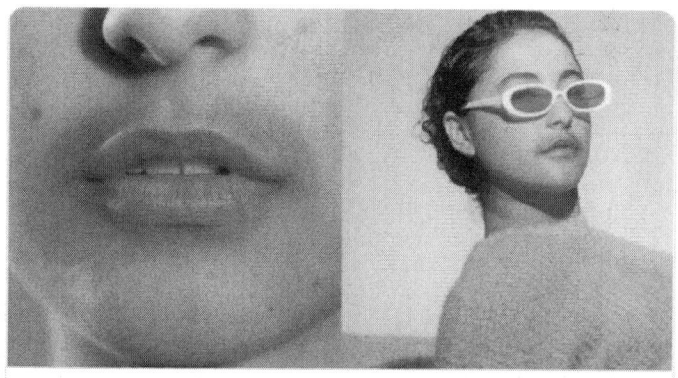

Billie's New Campaign Is the First Women's Razor Ad to Show Facial Hair
And it's for a good cause.
🔗 glamour.com

WHAT IT TAKES TO GO VIRAL

Image Source: moondustagency.com

Sometimes simplicity conquers all, even with viral content (think of the egg on Instagram example). The last thing you want to do is create your own roadblocks to writing regular content, and even though more in-depth content (such as story based content) will build better rapport with your audience, posting something is better than nothing.

Think about going to the gym and applying that same analogy to creating content. If you only go once per week or less, then you won't see the true benefits. However, if you go more frequently but do shorter or less intense sessions, that's of greater benefit. Whilst your next post probably won't be a hit right away, this shows you the real power of social media.

Viral videos are most definitely entertaining, however bear in mind that they can take a lot of time and money if you are trying to 'manufacture' them. They also don't always generate leads or customers for your business, which should always be your main objective with social media.

CHAPTER 14.

HOW TO SCALE YOUR BUSINESS UP

One thing that is important to do, is to track your engagement. As you start to build up engagement, I recommend creating a Business Facebook page. You can't improve what you don't measure. Business pages provide you with great engagement tracking that you don't get with your normal personal profile. The statistics are quite detailed and give you valuable information such as the demographics of your audience. The more you know about your audience and how engaged they are with your content, the easier it is to create compelling content.

Also, you have the ability to scale up your business further by using Facebook adverts on a Business Page. This isn't something I'll cover in a lot of detail in this book because you won't need this method on day one. It's very different from what we've been talking about with social media, so be prepared to switch gears.

That said, it's something you will want to consider as a long-term strategy, and some business owners reading this will already have the budget to test it. It also takes time to build up a new Business Page, and without an advertising budget it will take significantly longer. Also, you might exhaust your existing audience at some point, and running Facebook adverts is a quick way to keep yours growing.

I don't want to set you up for failure; however, I DO want you to maximize your social media potential. If your business is fairly new, then you will be running before you can walk at this point.

As you grow and scale your business, refer back to this information as it will certainly be useful. Just like the old saying goes 'when the student is ready the teacher appears'.

So, because of that, I will touch on these briefly because in the long term they are very important, and by not doing these you could be leaving money on the table. Along with this I'll cover another method to continue building your audience:

1) Facebook advertising (a.k.a. ads)

You can get started right away with Facebook advertising (ads), all you need to do is create an advertising account via your existing profile. There are no barriers to entry, other than your business model must be allowed to advertise on Facebook and you agree to follow their advertising terms.

If your business is allowed and your ads are approved, you can expect to start getting traffic within the hour. It is the fastest way to get targeted traffic to your website or offer that I can recommend.

I don't recommend using Facebook advertising until a) you have exhausted your existing audience and b) have at least a few hundred pounds per month to spend for at least three months. Otherwise you won't be maximising its use and your expectations may not be met.

Also, Facebook will be pushing you to 'Boost' your posts if you are posting on a Business Page. Do not do this no matter how enticing they try to make it, because this is only optimised for engagement. It is not optimised to get you leads, customers and sales.

Facebook has a lot of advertising goals but for most businesses just starting with Facebook ads, I only recommend two advert objectives:

1. **Videos** - for engagement

2. **Conversions** - for lead generation

Video ads are the most cost-effective way to get engagement and are cheaper than Boosting your posts. You could be paying less than 1p per view for targeted traffic (some of my clients are paying 0.1p per video view!). That's right, 10 targeted views for just 1p. Never has it been so affordable, simple, and instantaneous to advertise your business online.

Conversion ads have a few purposes. They are used to generate leads and build your email list (more on this in the next chapter). Conversions can also be used for generating sales, one example which you may have seen is if you have visited sites like Amazon, eBay or Wish and not purchased anything. This is known as an Abandoned Cart advert. Facebook also has their own code that they call a Pixel, which is used to track the effectiveness of your ads. You need to install the Pixel on your website to properly track any Conversion ads.

Even if you don't yet have a website or landing page (I'll explain what that is shortly if you're unaware) to send people to, you can still run Facebook ads to videos or other content you've created to get exposure. You can use a Facebook Business Page in the meantime, and I know many people who have grown their business without a website at all. Especially businesses that sell over the phone or in person.

The real power of Facebook ads is the retargeting aspect; where you can advertise to people that have visited your website (including checkout pages), Facebook page or content, joined your email list and a variety of other audience options.

You can even give Facebook a list of your customers for example, and it will find an audience using the data you have given to find a similar audience, but a much larger one.

Additionally, as I mentioned earlier in the book, you can target your competition. You can simply just tell Facebook the names of the big brands that you are up against and they will find their followers. For example, you can target people who like 'Nike' or 'Burger King'. It's all legitimate and these companies don't even know you are doing it.

It does however still require regular content creation - there are no shortcuts! However, you won't need to create new content as regularly if you're constantly advertising, because new people will see your ads every day.

Additionally, it's ultra-rare to post an advert and right away get results. I have made it happen before but it's uncommon and not to be expected, no matter how good you think your product or service is.

The other downside is that your account may get shut down if you keep getting adverts disapproved by Facebook's review team. You can even get your account shut down if you're running adverts that are approved but not performing well (they call these 'low quality' ads). This is quite promising as an advertiser, because the harder it is to advertise on a platform the better the audience quality. If you think about it, would you stick around on Facebook if you had irrelevant, hard to read or just plain annoying adverts you didn't want to see?

Let's say that you do make some mistakes and you do get your advertising account shut down, never fear as you can easily open a new one. Facebook staff have even advised me of this, even though they apparently do not open shut down accounts. However, if your profile that you use to create the advertising account is shut down, you can no longer open new accounts. You can appeal either of these decisions, but it is highly unlikely your account will be restored. Yes, it's a bizarre system and oftentimes they don't tell you the exact nature of an account being closed. They will just say it's against their Terms of Service and it can even happen by accident, so be prepared for it.

There is a good chance that the audience you advertise to will need to see a few of your ads before taking any interest. It is so important to test multiple pieces of content and ads to see which gets the most response. The cool thing about this is that advertising on social media platforms means your ads can get engagement. People will even start to share your ad with others if it really resonates with them.

Here is an example:

[Facebook ad screenshot: HubSpot Sponsored — "A CRM made for the way people sell today." Image reads "100% Free, Forever." HUBSPOT.COM — HubSpot Free CRM — All-in-one, completely free. Sign Up. You, David Downes, Lucy Douglas and 11K others. 1.8K comments 1.5K shares.]

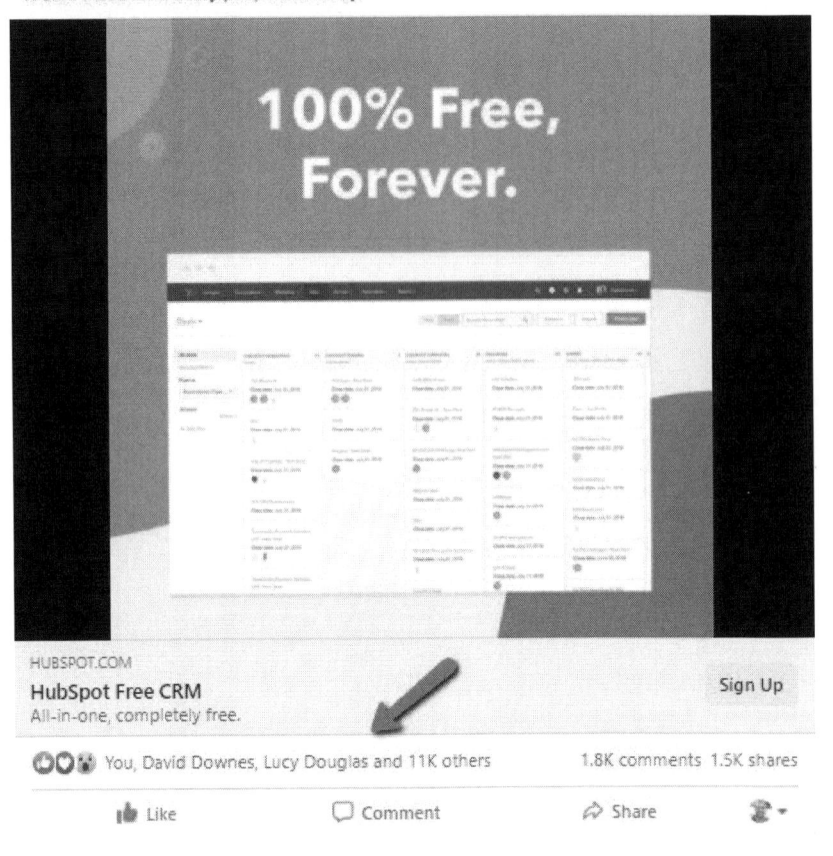

Nope, Hubspot are most certainly not going to win the award for the most interesting advert description of the year. I almost fell asleep reading it. It's also hard to make out what exactly is in the image. However, they are a well-known brand and the targeting is probably good, so they can get away with it. They've likely also been running the ad for a long time, which explains the high level of likes, comments, and shares.

Here's something a little more engaging for a few reasons - some might be more obvious to you than others.

Let's break this advert down:

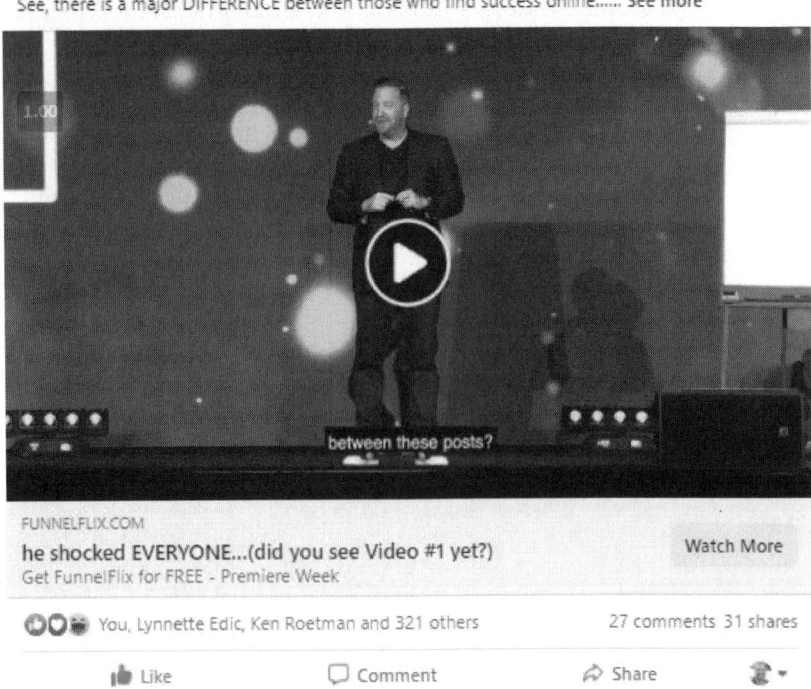

First, a question is asked straight away which increases the chances of engagement. There is also a longer description that tells you about the ad before having to watch the video.

The reason why the engagement is lower than the other advert is because the audience size for this advert is smaller, but more targeted. The advert might be brand new, so engagement alone isn't a deciding factor as to whether an advert is working well or not.

How do I know this? If you click on the 3 dots in the right-hand corner, Facebook will give you more information about the targeting used by the advertiser. It will look something like this:

> **Why you're seeing this ad**
> 🔒 Only you can see this
>
> You're seeing this ad because your information matches **ClickFunnels's** advertising requests. There could also be more factors not listed here. **Learn More**
>
> 💼 ClickFunnels used a list to reach you. >
>
> 🖼 ClickFunnels is trying to reach people aged 18 and older. >
>
> 📍 ClickFunnels is trying to reach people whose primary location is the United Kingdom. >

When it says 'Clickfunnels is using a list', the word "list" means what is called a Custom Audience, which is an audience such as an email list you can upload to Facebook. When setting up an ad you can choose an audience on Facebook or select your own customised audience.

The most important thing to remember is to keep an eye on your spending, especially early on in the campaign. Don't keep running ads that aren't bringing you a return. You do need to test multiple ads but not all of them will convert - you may find that you need to run 10 ads to get 2 providing any return.

However, if you can master the art of getting sales from Facebook ads, you have a huge edge. Your ads will then pay for themselves. It would be like putting £1 into a machine and getting £2 back, as many times as you wanted to. Yes, it does require an upfront investment and no return is guaranteed. However, it is a way to get immediate, targeted traffic.

If you can run ads for longer than your competition can, there is a good chance you can get your fair share of traffic, leads and sales from Facebook ads. Of course, this is easier said than done if you're on a strict budget! So, don't go into Facebook ads if you are going to be stopping and starting ads because it will not work. Especially if you already have a well engaged audience to tap into first.

One other important thing to map out, is to consider what I call your 'Product Ladder' is, before you ever promote anything via Facebook ads. This should be done with any paid advertising campaign or you will find it hard to generate a return. You may be spending money that may never return or may take a long time to turn a profit.

Your Product Ladder is basically all of your products you offer. You should start with at least three offers - a low priced offer (around £100), a mid-priced offer (around £500) and a high-priced offer (£1500+). Eventually you might want to add in more offers, especially higher priced premium offers, but let's keep it simple for now.

The reason you want to add in higher priced products is to cover the cost of your Facebook ads. If you understand your metrics, you could break even with your advertising or even lose money on the front end, but this would be fine because you can recoup your investment via a high priced product later on.

2) Build an email list by driving traffic to a landing page.
This is a slightly more advanced method that may require some tech assistance but is still something

that won't take a long time to set up. You will need a landing page builder, which is like a website but only has one call to action such as filling out a form on a website. It's optimised to get a specific result, rather than a website which tries to get the site visitor to do lots of things. Here is one example:

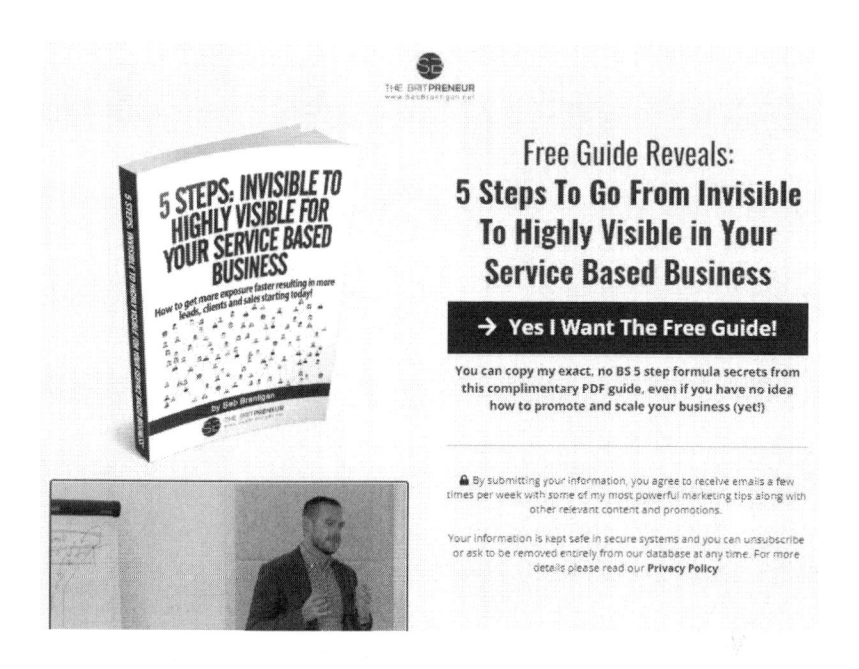

Then when someone clicks on the 'Yes I Want The Free Guide' they see this pop up:

THE BRITPRENEUR
www.SebBrantigan.net

Enter Your Best Email to Grab Your Guide:

Your Email Address Here...

Yes! Send Me The Guide

🔒 By submitting your information, you agree to receive emails a few times per week with some of my most powerful marketing tips along with other relevant content and promotions.

Your information is kept safe in secure systems and you can unsubscribe or ask to be removed entirely from our database at any time. For more details please read our Privacy Policy

(And no, we won't be pushing any upsells on the next page...)

You will also need an autoresponder, which is an online software that lets you send emails in batches easily and stores your leads. These are very inexpensive and not too complicated to set up - and even better, all of this is set-and-forget kind of stuff, too. They do however need to be set up the right way to ensure your emails actually get delivered and don't end up in your leads' junk or spam inbox. So, once you're up and running there's not a lot of ongoing maintenance needed.

Again, if you're reading this and it's making your head spin then it's probably something you should come back to or get some advanced help with. It is important to scale your business up, but this should be done only at a certain level.

Scaling up too early can distract you, cost you money and sink your business if you can't keep the main thing the main thing. Don't rush this process, as it is important to remember if one major component is out of line with the technical side it could render the whole task pointless.

When I used to do Judo, for example, I learnt that there are different levels you must achieve in order to progress to the next rank. You won't become a black belt overnight and you must master the basics first before building on them. You also wouldn't take on other black belts unless you were training with them.

All you need to do is to trust the process and stick with it. It may seem like an uphill struggle to get the ball rolling and to get results, however being able to build a responsive audience on social media is entirely possible.

For some people it can take weeks to see results, for others it may take months. Everyone and every business is different, so patience is a virtue. The reason why most people don't get any results on social media is they give up. It's a real shame because most are so close to victory, they could be one post or interaction away from attracting that dream client or customer.

Also bear in mind that people need to know, like and trust you before buying from you so this takes time. This is especially true if you have a higher priced or more complicated product or service, that may require more explanations or commitments before someone purchases. If you're in an industry like mine (digital marketing) there's also a high amount of scepticism which is important to factor in.

The rewards however can be unimaginable, such as always having an audience you can tap into at any time. Want to advertise a new offer? You have an audience for that. Want to build an email list? That's right you guessed it; you can ask your social media followers to subscribe to it. Need to raise money for a good cause? Your audience has your back (so long as you have theirs). Email marketing has worked for many years and is still a viable way to get eyeballs on your business or offer. Some people will tell you differently, but I use email marketing almost daily and have done so for years. I wouldn't be doing that unless it gets results (which it still does).

So many of us don't persist with what we really need to do and stay within our comfort zone. We're actually afraid of success or results and what that means, such as more drama and stress. We don't know if we can handle it or cope with it. Success, however, waits for us at the other side if we can ever leave our comfort zone. The question is, will you do something different to gain something different?

CHAPTER 15.

YOUR NEXT STEPS

Now I realise that this is a lot to process, remember and implement if this is all new to you. Creating and posting good quality content will take some getting used to, but you will start to see the benefits over time.

What's the biggest thing that stops people from using social media consistently?

Quite simply it's fear of the unknown, or fear of being judged. They may believe that nobody will listen to the content they put out there. Or their Auntie they haven't spoken to in 11 years will leave a snide comment, and possibly unfriend them. Yes, we've all been there, but could you imagine if everyone that received criticism let it get to them and never took any further action? There would be little innovation and success in the world.

I've learnt that right before a big breakthrough and results comes a lot of resistance, to the point that you think what you're doing is pointless or a waste of time. In most cases this isn't true, and you just need to try again with even more enthusiasm.

On top of that there's often a voice in our heads, saying things like "nobody is going to engage with this content post" or "this post is too short/too long" and all kinds of stories we make up in our minds. Life can also get in the way, sometimes our plans and schedules get interrupted, making it difficult to get back on course.

Long story short, you won't be able to grow your business with all the content ideas still in your head or only jotted on your notepad. You need to get out there and make you and your story known. Otherwise you'll just become another one of the world's best kept secrets!

I've already talked about this but remember to stay focused. Consider why you bought and opened this book in the first place. Trust me I have been there when it comes to being unfocused. Do you think I sat down to write this book and did not get distracted at all? A thousand and one things have come up since this book was started, but guess what, I still finished it. We all have just 24 hours in a day to finish what we need to, no matter how successful you become.

Let me use this book as an example. Being my first book, it was hard to see the end result, and I decided not to hire a ghostwriter simply because I didn't know what to give them. Even in school I don't think you'd have ever seen me write more than a few thousand words for one essay or exam. I'm not a natural writer or able to type 150 words per minute. I had some brilliant help with the editing and formatting but the rest was up to me. As a result, it's been quite the process putting this together, but I still made it happen.

Yes, I did tons of research into the subject but as you've guessed, the research alone isn't going to write the book. You won't be able to lose weight just by reading diet recipes or workout plans. At some point you need to stop researching and start doing to really learn everything you need to know. Putting pen to paper is what made it happen. I've rewritten or removed paragraphs that when I first wrote I thought would be perfect to include. It certainly has been a process that was tough to follow at times, even with the right guidance from others who had published books and online articles or blog posts. Eventually I stopped over analysing what was being written or it would never get published.

The longer I left the book outstanding, the harder it would be to finish it. My point here is that none of the process was perfect, but I kept going, at the risk that nobody would like or even read my book. Like running my online business, there were a million and one reasons to give up. Most days I did want to throw in the towel, but what kept me going is the freedom that running a digital business (or marketing your business digitally) can bring you. In this case I know there is a huge amount of useful information in this book to use for business owners, solopreneurs and anyone looking to promote themselves on social media.

It's far more than any 9 to 5 or traditional business can offer, although I'm not against either of these as a source of income. What kept me going was seeing others make it happen, and knowing it was possible if I kept going like they did. You have to just have the mindset that you know your craft, and you have something useful to share, to add to the marketplace. Otherwise you will overthink everything and not take enough action. Your best bet is to get into the mindset that you don't mind making mistakes, as long as you are making progress. We only have so many hours in a day and we can't spend it in a mode of what is called 'analysis paralysis'.

Anyway, you now have the complete formula I have used to build a full-time online business, meaning you could do the same as me or even exceed my results. At this point I've given you everything I can think of to get up and running, but nobody can do the work for you. Even if you hire an agency to do your social media, you will still need to supply them with information about your business and your strategy. There truly is no shortcut.

Like anything it can be outsourced, however a tip I'd like to share when it comes to outsourcing is to ensure that you already know a good amount about the task. It still pays to know the process well, so you know if the agency you hire is on track or not. You don't have to be an expert, especially if you are hiring such, but it's still your business at the end of the day so you may need to take the lead on the overall strategy. I'm not saying to micromanage - because that's not fun - and no way to run a business but DO educate yourself constantly as if you were doing it yourself.

My one request before we end our journey together, is to make a commitment today that you will follow these steps consistently. This won't work if you 'try' to apply this for a few days and then give up. One of my business mentors early on in my career, Jeffery Combs, said "the word 'try' means tomorrow is really yesterday" which is exactly what people do.

So, this is your opportunity to use all the information and strategies in this book to get more exposure for your brand or business. This is the point of the book where I would wish you good luck, however I'm a believer that luck is preparation meeting opportunity. I don't know about you, but I create my own luck, and nobody can do it for me!

So, what should you do as soon as you have finished this book?

My best advice would be to just make a start and get into a rhythm of content creation. This is probably the hardest part of the book - implementation! Not only that, but it's hard to continually do this. Most people will give up very easily and if life gets in the way, they will lose focus and end up forgetting where they got to. Then they start over with a new strategy, losing all progress. They are essentially spinning their wheels and won't ever build anything meaningful because they don't finish anything. The question is, are you like most people? As my old mentor used to say when he was encouraging people to go through his training programmes, "don't be a tool, use the tools!".

Want to know one productivity tip that will often ensure I get something important done? If it's something important I will put down the task as a reminder in my smartphone calendar. You may wish to do this first thing in the morning, so that it's done and out of the way. I recommend doing this for your phone too, by putting something like "content post" as a daily recurring task.

That way you will see it above to do lists, post-it notes etc. especially if you change your phone settings so the reminder flashes on your phone. To be honest, when I set a reminder in this way, I would estimate the task gets done 80-90% of the time. Usually within the same hour!

One other 'hack' I can give you, if you have a tablet then buy a cheap stand for it (eBay sells them for a few pounds) and stand it up on your desk so it faces you. Make sure the screen stays on for some time whilst your tablet is idle. Put your to do list on there using a project management tool like Trello, and there won't be any escaping it!

One mistake I've made in the past is having a plan in my head but never noting anything down. You might find a bullet point list of actions works for you or drawing diagrams or flowcharts might be your thing. Otherwise it's just another great idea that takes up bandwidth in your head but doesn't do much else. Successful people take notes and write important things down. Imagine your notes as uncashed cheques, you would be much more likely to put them into action then!

If you're feeling a bit uninspired then just pick up this book and read through it once more. I can almost guarantee you'll pick up something you missed last time. Just follow the four P.I.M.P. steps consistently and refer back to them as much as you need to. There have been a number of books, like Mike Dillard's Magnetic Sponsoring book I mentioned, that having re-read them have given me a huge amount of new insight. Maybe you've had the same experience. Social Marketing Success is a resource you can use if you're getting stuck or something isn't working. Often times going back to basics is the best way to figure out how to move forward.

Lastly, if having read my book you have gained some useful insights, I would like to invite you to leave me a review on Amazon, helping the book get seen by more people. If you need to find it, please search for 'Social Marketing Success by Seb Brantigan' to visit the Amazon book page, with the review section lower down on the page.

BONUS SECTION
COMPLIMENTARY SAMPLE COACHING BY THE BRITPRENEUR

Also, as a thank you for finishing the book I wanted to offer you yet another complimentary gift - a 'sample' of coaching from me. You may email me any business-related question completely for free over email, with this email coaching limited to one question per person. This isn't something I have offered before so depending on how it goes, I may or may not do it again in future! Thus, my advice is not to pass this offer up.

Email seb@sebbrantigan.net, with the subject line 'Social Marketing Success' and with your burning question clearly written. There is no maximum length for a question but trying to disguise three questions into one won't get it answered!

Additionally, if you would like to leave a testimonial or feedback about something you've learnt from me or the book, you can also do so using the above email address. Please note that by sending me feedback you give me permission to use it in my marketing, including your name (include your company name for free exposure).

I believe in you and your ability to go out and create your own luck - you CAN do this. Let me know your progress along the way and be sure to reference this book several times if you get stuck. It could be the difference between success or failure in your business.

Best wishes,

Seb Brantigan

'The Britpreneur'

RESOURCES

Unannounced Bonus Resource - Free Strategy Session

If you would like some assistance from me to implement the strategies taught in this book to ensure you get the results you want, I'd like to invite you to book your free strategy session. You can do this using the below link:

https://sebbrantigan.net/bookacall

Or if you'd like to get your social media and digital marketing set up for you, totally hands free? You can also speak to me about hiring my team to get something custom built for your business. Simply book in a free strategy session using the link above.

*****

Here's a list of some useful resources mentioned in Social Marketing Success.

Disclaimer: for full transparency, some of the following tools do contain affiliate links and I may receive a commission if you decide to purchase through them. If you are in a mood to 'reciprocate' then please use the links below, otherwise you can Google the below resources for non-affiliate links (I won't lose sleep over it if you do!)

Upwork - Hire people per hour to assist with content creation and management.

https://www.upwork.com/

Fiverr - Hire people on a one-off cost or project basis. I currently use Fiverr for basic graphics design such as book covers, digital course graphics and photo editing. Turnaround is very quick but from experience if you are not clear in your initial instructions you may receive something very different from what you expected!

https://sebbrantigan.net/fiverr

Hootsuite - Lets you schedule out multiple pieces of content onto multiple social media platforms. Perfect if you want to get organised with your content and remain consistent with posting.

https://hootsuite.com/

Clickfunnels - Create high converting, fully customisable websites, sales funnels, membership sites and products within minutes. I genuinely have not found a better capture page creation software on the market, and it's one of my most used tools.

http://sebbrantigan.net/clickfunnels

ActiveCampaign - Send emails, create automated email marketing campaigns and organise your email list. This is a necessary tool to take list building, segmenting and automation to the next level. Ideal for list building and email marketing beginners.

http://sebbrantigan.net/activecampaign

Infusionsoft - All In One Customer Relationship Manager software. It's like ActiveCampaign but with more features, such as allowing you to take payments, lead scoring, sales prospecting tools and a lot more. I only recommend this tool for medium to large sized businesses only.

https://sebbrantigan.net/infusionsoftdemo

*****

I also have a more extensive list of resources and tools for your business on my website:

https://sebbrantigan.net/resources

If you've enjoyed reading this book, the perfect extension of Social Marketing Success is my **Social Marketing Success Bootcamp**.

Inside the Bootcamp you'll find 6 modules on how to get more leads, clients and sales with the power of social media. I'll also give you my best resources, tools and documents to master these platforms to get more leads and sales for your business.

As a reader of Social Marketing Success, you can get access to the Bootcamp for 50% off the retail price. You can become a member of the Social Marketing Success Bootcamp for a one-time investment of £97.

Here is what you get by becoming a member:

Module 1 - Fast Track to Getting Started On Social Media

Module 2 - Knowing Your Market

Module 3 - How to Turn Engagement Into Leads

Module 4 - Turning Social Leads Into Social Customers

Module 5 - Building a Thriving, Lasting Audience on Social

Module 6 - Scaling Up & Automating Your Social Results

More details about the Social Marketing Success Bootcamp and enrolling can be found via the below link: https://sebbrantigan.net/smsbootcamp

Testimonials from attendees of my previous training sessions or courses:

"We have been friends for over a year now. This is a guy who is straight to the point, with a no BS approach when it comes to marketing. Seb has an awesome knowledge of the online marketing industry and is one of the first people I mastermind with. Always has some great value to offer. A top guy you should definitely connect with if you want to discover how to grow your business online, with any marketing strategy!" Matt Richards, Social Media Expert and Online Business Coach

"I've had the pleasure of not only knowing Seb for years but working with him on many successful projects. It's not a surprise so many businesses seek his expertise in setting up and scaling marketing campaigns to increase sales and revenue. If you're looking for someone to help you build your business online, you're in the right place with Seb." -Phil Faulkner, Business Success and Sales Coach

"Just wanted to say a big thank you for the advice you gave me on social media. You gave me the confidence to step out of my comfort zone and be active. Appreciate it!" -Michelle O'Mahony

Printed in Great Britain
by Amazon